Okinawa: capstone to victory

Okinawa: capstone to victory

Benis M Frank

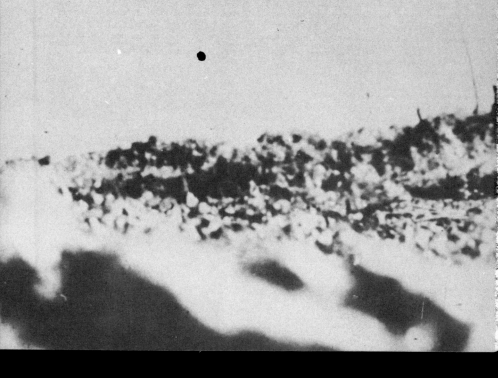

Editor-in-Chief: Barrie Pitt
Art Director: Peter Dunbar

Military Consultant: Sir Basil Liddell Hart
Picture Editor: Bobby Hunt

Executive Editor: David Mason
Designer: Sarah Kingham
Cover: Denis Piper
Research Assistant: Yvonne Marsh
Cartographer: Richard Natkiel
Special Drawings: John Batchelor

Photographs for this book were especially selected from the following Archives: from left to right
6-7 Imperial War Museum; 9 IWM; 12 US Army; 12-13 US Navy; 12 US Navy; 13 Associated
Press; 14-15 US Air Force; 16 Marine Corps; 20-21 US Navy; 22-23 US Navy; 24-25 US Navy; 26-27 US Army;
29 US Navy; 30-31 IWM; 32-33 IWM; 34 Marine Corps; 36-37 Keystone Tokyo; 38 Marine Corps; 40-41 US Navy
40 US Navy; 45 US Navy/US Army; 47-48 US Navy; 50-51 US Navy; 54 Marine Corps; 54-55 Marine Corps; 58-59
US Navy/US Army; 60-61 Marine Corps; 63 Marine Corps/US Navy; 64 Marine Corps; 65 US Navy/Marine Corps;
68-69 Marine Corps; 71 US Army; 74-75 Marine Corps; 74 Marine Corps; 76-77 IWM; 76 IWM; 78-79 IWM; 81 US
Navy; 82 US Navy; 83 Marine Corps/US Army; 86-87 US Navy; 90 Marine Corps; 92 US Navy; 94 Marine Corps;
95 US Army; 96-97 Marine Corps; 97 US Navy; 98 Marine Corps; 99 Marine Corps; 101 IWM; 102-103 US Army;
102 Marine Corps; 106-107 Marine Corps; 108-109 US Navy; 109 Marine Corps; 110 Marine Corps; 111 Marine
Corps; 112 US Army; 113 IWM; 114-115 Marine Corps; 118-119 Marine Corps; 121 Marine Corps; 122-123 Marine
Corps; 127 Marine Corps; 130-131 Marine Corps; 133 Marine Corps; 134-135 Marine Corps; 137 Marine Corps;
142-143 US Army; 144-145 Marine Corps; 147 IWM; 148 US Navy; 150-151 US Army; 153 Marine Corps; 155 US
Navy; 159 Marine Corps.

Contents

The day of the Kamikazes

Introduction by Barrie Pitt

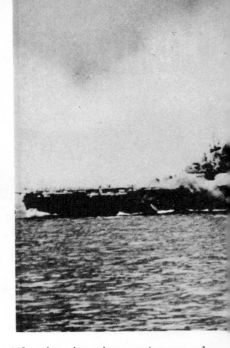

There was never any doubt that the battle for Okinawa would be amongst the bitterest and bloodiest of the war. From the point of view of the Japanese defenders, there was no illusion that it was anything except the last battle before the invasion of the homeland itself – and their code of military honour ensured that whatever else may be in short supply, there would be no lack of that stubborn bravery which had already astonished the military world.

From the point of view of the attackers, Okinawa was the culmination of four years of the Pacific War. The commanders and most of the forces were well seasoned; the naval, air and ground doctrines had been through trial by fire in the far reaches of the Pacific and tempered thus to an unparalleled expertise, and American war industry had reached a peak which ensured that no material shortage would hinder the Allied advance. It is probably true to say that no military force in history went into action better equipped and better supported than General Buckner's Tenth Army.

The scene was set, therefore, for a clash of Homeric proportions – and one can appreciate the feelings of the battle-wise American veterans who made up the first assault groups, when 50,000 of them were allowed by the defenders to establish themselves on the beaches virtually without casualty. Many undoubtedly reflected that if it was Easter Sunday, it was also All Fool's Day; and bitter disillusionment must soon come to the over-optimistic.

In fact, it was nearly nine days before the Americans came up against the hard defensive crust which General Ushijima, and his indefatigable Chief of Staff General Cho, had constructed across the southern end of the island, and the infantrymen and Marines of General Hodges' XXIV Corps got their first intimation of what they were in for. After a bombardment by twenty-seven battalions of artillery (324 guns) augmented by the fire power of six battleships, six cruisers and six destroyers, and the strike capacity of 650 Navy and Marine planes (altogether 19,000 artillery shells were fired in forty minutes), a three-divisional attack went in – and failed to break the first line.

Thus began a period of eighty days during which defenders and attackers fought each other with a fury and

desperation seldom equalled and never surpassed. The honeycomb of defensive positions gave the Japanese great advantages in which their courage and devotion were exploited to the full; American technology gave the attackers the 'blowtorch and corkscrew' hardware without which all the aggressive valour in the world would have been to no avail. And from the records of those eighty days, Benis Frank, already the author of the official Marine Corps operational history of the battle, has now distilled a fine account of the conflict, illustrated, as will be seen, by magnificent action photographs taken by the highly skilled Marine Corps photographers.

Because of limitations of space, however, there is one aspect of the Okinawa campaign that I feel the author has somewhat overlooked. This period was the zenith of the Japanese Kamikaze attack, when their *tokko tai* pilots made the supreme effort. Several Allied ships were hit during the approach voyage to Okinawa, 355 suicide missions were flown on April 6th and 7th against the huge fleet anchored off the beaches, and at the same time the biggest

Dreadnought battleship ever to be built, the Japanese *Yamato*, was sent on a one-way trip to immolate herself in a similar self-sacrificial action.

It is insensitive and unwise to dismiss such tactics as wasteful and such attitudes as made it possible as mere fanaticism. So far as their effectiveness was concerned, of the 1,900 suicide missions actually flown during the battle for Okinawa, it is calculated that 14.7 per cent were effective – which is a thoroughly acceptable proportion in any form of warfare – and at one time during April some American naval officers were beginning to think that the kamikazes would successfully interrupt the invasion.

So far as the charge of fanaticism is concerned, such casuistry begs the question. The young men who flew their aircraft or their *Okha* bombs into the decks of Allied ships did so because they believed in the rightness and justice of their cause, and were willing to give their lives to advance that cause in the slightest degree.

What else is bravery and devotion to duty?

Approach to Iceberg

Like so many of the other scenes of Allied assault operations in the Pacific, before the Second World War Okinawa was known only perhaps to geographers, historians, and maybe crossword puzzle fans. While both the Joint and Combined Chiefs of Staff became vitally interested in this area of the Japanese Empire when the war began – and earlier – it was not until after they had chosen Okinawa as a major target and firmly scheduled its invasion date that the full force of Allied intelligence and operational planning was focused on this, the major island of the Ryukyu Retto.

The selection of Okinawa as a target stemmed almost directly from decisions reached at the Sextant Conference in Cairo in 1943, when President Roosevelt and Prime Minister Churchill established a timetable for the prosecution of the Pacific War. In accordance with their decisions a coordinated, converging, two-pronged drive was mounted across the Central Pacific and up from the Southwest Pacific to gain bases from which attacks were to be launched against Formosa, Luzon, and the China coast in the spring of 1945.

General Douglas MacArthur, Commander-in-Chief Southwest Pacific Area, directed the first drive along the northern coast of New Guinea and then headed for the Philippines. In the second approach axis, the forces of Admiral Chester W Nimitz, Commander-in-Chief Pacific Ocean Areas (CinCPOA), pushed through the Central Pacific to the core of enemy island outposts which defended the heart of the Japanese Empire. In the course of both drives, major elements of the Pacific Fleet – Nimitz wore a second hat as Commander-in-Chief, Pacific Fleet (CinCPac) – supported specifically assigned amphibious operations within the strategic command areas of both MacArthur and Nimitz. Other elements of the Fleet contained Japanese surface and air forces at the same time.

The unexpectedly rapid success of Allied operations in 1944, however, required that the Sextant Plan be reviewed, and perhaps revised as well. Regardless of the number of other desirable and attainable options which appeared feasible in lieu of the Formosan invasion, Sextant quite clearly stipulated Formosa as a major objective. Therefore, in March 1944 the Joint Chiefs of Staff issued a directive which, among other things, required Nimitz – as CinCPOA – to prepare plans for Operation Causeway, an amphibious assault against Formosa scheduled for early 1945. At the same time, the JCS directive assigned MacArthur the responsibility for planning the recapture of Luzon, 'should such operations prove necessary prior to the move on Formosa.'

For Causeway, Nimitz placed Admiral Raymond A Spruance, com-

mander of both the Fifth Fleet and the Central Pacific Task Forces, in overall charge of the operation. He had already achieved an outstanding record in the war as leader of the US carrier force which decisively defeated the Japanese fleet at the Battle of Midway in June 1942. Since that time, he had headed up the forces which landed on Tarawa and the Marshalls, and it was his Fifth Fleet which so thoroughly destroyed Japanese naval strength in the Battle of the Philippine Sea in June 1944.

Spruance's principal amphibious commander for Causeway was Vice-Admiral Richmond Kelly Turner, who was to lead the expeditionary forces. Like Spruance, Turner was a fully experienced naval officer who, as Director, War Plans Division, in the Office of the Chief of Naval Operations in 1940-1942, planned many of the operations in which he was a direct participant. He had commanded the amphibious forces at Guadalcanal and New Georgia in the Solomons campaigns, in the Gilberts, the Marshalls (as Commander, Southern Attack Force, under Spruance), and at Saipan. Turner's expertise in planning for and conducting amphibious assaults was considerable, and his reputation as a hard-driving, no-nonsense naval martinet was legendary.

Assigned to command the Expeditionary Troops and the Tenth Army was Lieutenant-General Simon

Three power conference in North Africa. Seated, left to right: Marshal Chiang Kai Shek, President Roosevelt, Winston Churchill

Bolivar Buckner, Jr, USA, who, prior to this assignment, was the Commanding General, Alaskan Command. A compact, blue-eyed, gray-haired Army officer, and a member of the West Point Class of 1908, Buckner was the son of a Confederate general of some reputation in the Civil War. These, then, were the major commanders selected for Causeway.

Despite the fact that the planning for Causeway was well along, and the commanders and forces already designated, there was some doubt in the minds of certain senior officers as to its feasibility. Additionally, members of the American Joint War Plans Committee, who, among other things, were concerned with determining future Pacific strategy, had developed a comprehensive study exceeding in scope and perspective previous strategic planning. In effect, these Washington-based planners outlined a series of campaigns which would lead to an assault on Japan itself, with an amphibious landing to take place on the Kanto Plain at the head of Tokyo Bay. The Committee members assumed that the Allies could force Japan into suing for unconditional surrender by 'Lowering Japanese ability to resist by establishing sea

9

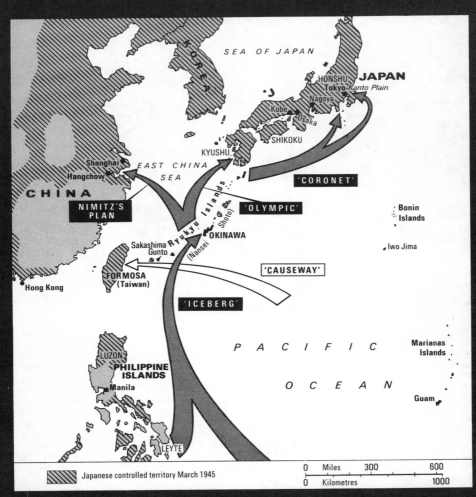

The Western Pacific. Projected Allied operations in early 1945

and air blockades, conducting intensive air bombardments and destroying Japanese air and naval strength' and by 'Invading and seizing the industrial heart of Japan.'

The Committee suggested that three phases precede the invasion of Japan. During the period 1st April-30th June 1945, American forces would seize positions in the Bonins and Ryukyus from which an invasion could be launched against the central China coast in the Hangchow Bay area. From 30th June to 30th September, Causeway troops would consolidate and initially exploit the China beachhead. Finally, Allied forces would land on southern Kyushu on 1st October (Operation Olympic) and on the Tokyo Plain of Honshu on 31st December (Operation Coronet).

In mid-July 1944, the JCS approved the general concepts of this recommended plan and agreed to have it presented at the Octagon Conference in Quebec in September. At the conference, Churchill and his advisers agreed to the new schedule only after they had been assured that no new operation would be undertaken in the Pacific which would lessen the priorities given to the war in Europe.

On 23rd August 1944, Nimitz published the Causeway Joint Staff Study, in which he stated that he intended invading Formosa after MacArthur's forces had firmly established positions in the south and central Philippines. Following the assault on Formosa, either the Ryukyus and the Bonins together or the China coast were to be invaded as a prelude to the attack on Japan itself. Not all of the American commanders in the Pacific were satisfied that it was practical, necessary, or possible to take Formosa, and this target became the center of some controversy and discussion, despite the fact that it had been all but firmly established as the scene of a future operation. General Buckner objected because of the shortage in the Pacific of available service and support troops for the Tenth Army and Causeway, and he assumed that the War Department would be unable to make up this deficit before the war in Europe ended. As a result, he recommended cancellation of Causeway, as did Lieutenant-General Millard F Harmon, commander of the Army Air Forces in the Pacific, who proposed instead amphibious assaults on the Bonins and the Ryukyus.

Another very senior officer who held similar views was Admiral Ernest J King, American Chief of Naval Operations and a member of the Joint Chiefs of Staff. On 2nd October 1944, he recommended to his fellow Joint Chiefs that operations be mounted successively against Luzon, Iwo Jima, and the Ryukyus. Agreeing, on 3rd October, the JCS directed MacArthur to invade Luzon on 20th December and Nimitz to land Marines on Iwo Jima exactly one month later, although the Iwo Jima operation did not come off until 19th February. Following these two operations, Iceberg, the invasion of Okinawa, was to take place on 1st March 1945.

Of necessity, the Iceberg date remained flexible because it was predicated on the timely completion of the Iwo Jima operation in order to permit the prompt release of the fire support surface elements and close air support squadrons for use at Okinawa. Other factors influencing the choice for an Okinawa invasion date were the similarly prompt release to Iceberg forces of the naval support forces and assault shipping used in the Luzon landing and attainment of complete and undisputed Allied control of the sea around and air above the target area following massive preliminary strikes against the Ryukyus, Formosa, Japan, and, of course, Okinawa itself.

Once having made the decision to invade Okinawa, the Joint Chiefs reserved the Formosan venture as a strategic goal for possible reconsideration at a later date. Fortunately, the basic command concept and structure, and the troop list organization established for Causeway, could be retained for Iceberg, and CinCPac-CinCPOA planners simply shifted the focus of their attention to the new target. In compliance with the JCS directive to Admiral Nimitz 'to occupy one or more positions in the Nansei Shoto' – another name for the Ryukyus – staff officers in Pearl Harbor began filling in the details of an outline plan for the operation.

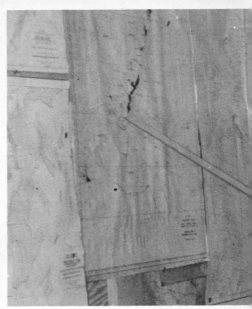

'Causeway' planners and commanders
Left: Lieutenant-General Simon B Buckner USA
Above: Vice-Admiral Richmond K Turner
Below: Admirals Ernest J King and Chester W Nimitz
Right: Admiral Raymond A Spruance

The target

Okinawa's strategic importance was derived from its location, and all other Allied and Japanese considerations were based on this factor. The island is an integral link in the Ryukyus chain, which, during the Second World War, formed an effective barrier to Allied advances from the east or southeast towards the Chinese mainland, Korea, and the western coast of Japan. Okinawa was a tempting and lucrative target to the Allies, for, as the largest island in the Ryukyus, its capture would provide them with an excellent base on which assault troops would stage and train for final operations against Japan.

The distances from Okinawa to other major target areas were slight. Kyushu was only 350 nautical miles away; Formosa 330 miles; and Shanghai 450 miles. In addition to its staging facilities, the island also had numerous airbase sites whose potential development meant more trouble

for Japan. Located in the Ryukyus were the only two substantial fleet anchorages between Kyushu and Formosa. Both of these anchorages were on the east coast of Okinawa; one was in Nakagusuku Wan (Bay) and the second in Chinen Wan.

Okinawa is the major island of the Okinawa Gunto, or Group. To the west of Okinawa and part of the Gunto also are Kume Shima, Aguni Shima, Ie Shima, and Kerama Retto; Iheya Retto and Yoron Shima in the north; and a group of smaller islands roughly paralleling the east central coast of Okinawa. These the Americans named the Eastern Islands. Before the end of the Iceberg operation, all of these islands were to be reconnoitered, and some, in fact, were to be occupied.

The island of Okinawa itself is irregularly shaped, sixty miles long, and has a breadth of eighteen miles at its greatest width, where Motobu

and the enemy

Peninsula juts out into the East China Sea. Two-thirds of the island's mass lies north of the Ishikawa Isthmus. The territory here is heavily wooded and mountainous, and is today unchanged from what it had been in 1945. The center portion of Okinawa – bounded on the north by the isthmus and on the south by a cross-island valley running between Naha and Yonabaru – consists of some steep cliffs, deep ravines, and gently rolling hills. Okinawa's southernmost portion is triangularly shaped, very hilly, and contains vast, 500-foot-high limestone plateaux. At each angle of the base of the triangle is a peninsula – Oroku on the west coast and Chinen on the east.

Like its interior, the island's coastline varies considerably, ranging from a precipitous and rocky shore in the north, through a reefbound, lowland belt just below Ishikawa Isthmus at the waist of the island, to an area of raised beaches and sea cliffs with sheer drops in the south. Few of the limited number of landing beaches on Okinawa were suitable for large-scale amphibious operations. On the east coast, the largest beaches and most extensive flatlands border Nakagusuku Wan, which was later named Buckner Bay in honor of the Tenth Army commander. On the opposite coast, the best beaches lay between Zampa Misaki and Oroku Peninsula.

Okinawa's road net was fair to nonexistent, although some decent highways existed in the Naha area, the most heavily populated section of the Island. In addition to coastal roads, a capillary network of paths, trails, and secondary roads branched inland from the coasts. During the dry season, the slightest movement on these roads would throw up a cloud of dust; during the rainy season, the roads and trails were sheer bogs for the most part.

The climate of Okinawa is tropical

15

Japanese Thirty-second Army chiefs at Okinawa. *Left to right:* Ota, Ushijima, Cho, Kanayama, Hongo, Yahara

in nature, and the island is often subject to heavy rainfall and typhoons most of which occur during the months July through November. In September 1945, the winds of one typhoon were clocked at 120 miles per hour.

The native Okinawans, most of whom were farmers, represent a complex Sino-Japanese racial mixture with a few other Asian strains thrown in over the years. The cultural impact of the Chinese was more pronounced, however, for as one Japanese soldier wrote in his notebook, 'the houses and customs here resemble those of China, and remind one of a Chinese town.' Eventually the Okinawan developed his own peculiar culture, and a religion which basically took the form of ancestor worship. Attesting to this fact are the thousands or horseshoe-shaped burial vaults, many of impressive size and quaint beauty, set into the sides of cliffs and hills throughout the island.

Until April 1944, when the Japanese Thirty-second Army was activated on the island and given responsibility for the defense of the Ryukyus, Okinawa remained in the backwash of the war for the most part. Prior to this date, the Japanese had paid little attention to bolstering their defenses in the Nansei Shoto. However, recognition of American successes in the Pacific and the peril threatening the Home Islands soon changed enemy attitudes and stirred the Japanese Imperial General Headquarters into action. One of the first moves of the IGHQ in Tokyo was to quickly repair the weaknesses in the Empire's inner defenses by expediting . . . operational preparations in the area extending from Formosa to the Nansei Islands with the view of defending our territory in the Nansei area and securing our lines of communication with our southern sector of operations . . .'

Stimulating Japanese defense efforts were American operations in the Central Pacific in mid-1944, and especially the fall of Saipan in July – which brought down the Tojo regime – and the landings on Peleliu and Morotai on 15th September 1944. By this time, the Japanese high command was certain that either Formosa, the Ryukyus, or the Bonins – or all three – were to be invaded by the spring of 1945 at the latest. In face of established American air superiority and the demonstrated weakness of Japanese air forces, the role of air in the defense of the Home Islands was downgraded. The ground forces, then, had to carry the entire burden alone, for even the once-vaunted Japanese navy was by 1945 a mere shadow of its former self. What slight strength the navy had remaining was being carefully hoarded at scattered ports throughout Japan and being held in readiness until it could be used against the US fleet in a 'decisive victory,' a term the enemy liked to employ though never really succeeded in accomplishing during the course of any surface engagement in the war.

In August 1944, Lieutenant-General Mitsuri Ushijima relieved the ailing Lieutenant-General Masao Watanabe, the first commander of the Thirty-second Army. Because of the importance it gave to the impending battle for Okinawa, IGHQ assigned as Chief of Staff to Ushijima, Major-General (later Lieutenant-General) Isamu Cho, one of the most competent officers in the Japanese Army. Ushijima and Cho formed a command team in which each officer's military expertise and personality complimented the other's. Their relationship reflected mutual trust and confidence.

A senior officer slated for promotion to general in August 1945, Ushijima was reputedly a man of great integrity and character who demonstrated quiet competence and in turn inspired great confidence, loyalty, and respect from his subordinates. In comparison, Cho was an extremely aggressive man with a reputation throughout the Army as a strict disciplinarian. Hard driving, he spared neither himself nor his staff. These two officers were ably abetted by the lone holdover from the old staff, Colonel Hiromichi Yahara, the senior operations officer.

Facing General Ushijima was an almost-impossible task and not too many experienced troops with whom he could accomplish it. Most of the Thirty-second Army's major reinforcing organizations arrived on Okinawa from their previous posts in China, Manchuria, and Japan between June and August 1944. The first to arrive was the 9th Infantry Division, a crack veteran unit and destined to be the backbone of Ushijima's defensive force. But he was not to be given the luxury of this division for long, however, because it was more urgently needed on Luzon after MacArthur's landings there. In December, the 9th left Okinawa for the Philippines by way of Formosa. Here it sat out the rest of the war, prevented by American planes and submarines from continuing the trip. Unfortunately for the Thirty-second Army commander, this division was never replaced by another nor were its troops replaced by other experienced, battle-tried

soldiers. The loss of this division from the Okinawa garrison was to have dire consequences for the Japanese on the course of the coming battle.

In June 1944, the Thirty-second Army was to have been reinforced by the 44th Independent Mixed Brigade, formed that same month on Kyushu. The ship carrying the brigade to Okinawa was torpedoed while en route, resulting in the loss of over 5,000 men, and only 600 survivors reached their destination. The following month, the 15th Independent Mixed Regiment was flown directly to Okinawa and added to the remnants of the 44th Brigade.

The next unit of any size to reach Okinawa was the 24th Infantry Division, which had previously been based in Manchuria. Well equipped and trained, it had not yet been blooded in battle. Before leaving for the Ryukyus, it had been stripped of personnel who were added to expeditionary forces sent out in early 1944 to the Pacific to reinforce other Japanese units. Not until the Thirty-second Army was reorganized in February 1945 was the division brought up to near its original strength. Nonetheless, with a total of 14,000 men, it was the largest tactical unit available to Ushijima.

Lieutenant-General Takeo Fujioka's 62nd Infantry Division was the final major infantry unit assigned to the Thirty-second Army. This was a brigaded division consisting of two brigades of four independent infantry battalions each. In mid-September 1944, two more of these battalions arrived on Okinawa and were parcelled out one to each brigade.

Because Imperial General Headquarters foresaw the battle of Okinawa as one of fixed defenses, Ushijima was not assigned any appreciably strong armored force. The 27th Tank Regiment, organised in April 1944 from elements of the 2nd Armored Division in Manchuria, joined the Thirty-second Army in July. One of the regiment's medium tank companies was sent to the Miyako Jima garrison. Remaining was an armored task force consisting of one light and one medium tank company, a tractor-drawn artillery battery, an infantry company, and other assorted support

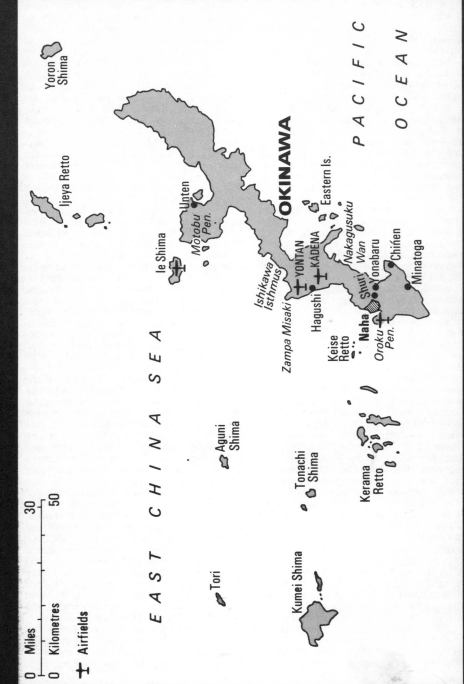

Okinawa and its neighbouring islands, the Okinawa Gunto

groups. The tanks' heaviest armament was a 57mm gun mounted on the mediums.

As a result of the hopeless situation facing Japanese units in the Philippines and the inability of Japanese shipping to deliver supplies and reinforcements, IGHQ diverted large weapons shipments – if not troops – to Okinawa. The Thirty-second Army thus possessed a heavier concentration of artillery under a single command than had been available to any other Japanese organization in the Pacific at any one time. Total enemy artillery strength on Okinawa, less the 42nd Field Artillery Regiment which was organic to the 24th Division, was grouped within the 5th Artillery Command. In addition to the comparatively weak 7th Heavy Artillery Regiment, Major-General Kosuke Wada's command consisted of two independent artillery regiments, a heavy artillery battalion, and the artillery elements of the 44th Brigade and the 27th Tank Regiment. In addition, he had the 1st and 23rd Medium Artillery Regiments with thirty-six howitzers, and the 100th Heavy Artillery Battalion with eight 150mm guns.

Wada also had under his command three of the six batteries of the 1st Independent Heavy Mortar Regiment, which fired 320mm spigot mortars, first encountered by the Americans on Iwo Jima. These fantastic weapons fired a 675-pound shell which the Marines irreverently dubbed a 'flying ashcan.' Although the 1st and 2nd Light Mortar Battalions were nominally part of Wada's organization, their ninety-six 81mm mortars were assigned in close support of the infantry and controlled by the defense sector commanders.

In addition to these regular organizations, Ushijima drew strength from other diverse and supporting elements. The reserve of potential infantry replacements on the island varied from good, in the 23rd and 26th Shipping Engineer Regiments, to poor at best in assorted rear area service units. The largest number of replacements, 7,000 men, was provided by the 19th Air Sector Command, comprised of airfield maintenance and construction units at the Yontan, Kadena, and Ie Shima air strips. Another source of infantry replacements were the seven sea raiding squadrons, three of which were based at Kerama Retto and the remainder at Unten-Ko in the north of Okinawa. Each of these squadrons had a hundred picked men, whose sole duty was to destroy American amphibious invasion shipping during the course of landing operations by crashing explosive-laden suicide craft into the sides of attack transports and cargo vessels.

Ushijima's naval component consisted of the Okinawa Naval Base Force, the 4th Surface Escort Unit, and various naval aviation activities, all under the command of Rear-Admiral Minoru Ota. In this combined command were approximately 9,000 men, only thirty-five percent of whom were regular naval personnel. The remaining men were civilian employees belonging to the different subunits of the Naval Base Force, but nonetheless considered to be part of the naval component. Part of Ota's command consisted of torpedo boat, suicide boat, and midget submarine squadrons at the Unten-Ko base on Motobu Peninsula. While the total naval strength was impressive, it really did not have a military potential commensurate with its size.

Rounding out the Thirty-second Army was a native Okinawan home guard, whose members were called *Boeitai*. A volunteer group, its equipment and training were provided by the Army, into whose ranks it was to be integrated once the battle for Okinawa was joined. It is estimated that the *Boeitai* provided Ushijima with 17,000-20,000 men. Added to this were 1,700 male Okinawan students, fourteen years of age and older, who were organized into volunteer youth groups – Blood and Iron for the Emperor Duty Units, or *Yekketsu*, as they were called in Japanese. These lads were to be assigned initially to communications units, but eventually joined frontline and guerrilla organizations after the island was invaded.

By the date of the American landings, Ushijima could fight a total of approximately 100,000 troops. He had some 67,000 men in the regular units of the Thirty-second Army, 9,000 troops in the Naval Base Force, and

The airfield on Ie Shima

about 24,000 Okinawans. Even before these men were to meet the Americans in combat, they had their work cut out for them in preparing the island's defenses.

The pattern of Allied assault operations in the Pacific was quite apparent to the Japanese by this time. No longer could they stand and fight at the beachhead with any hope of success, for American naval gunfire bombardments would just about destroy all shore defenses before troops ever hit the beaches, and any installation that was left standing after this pre-invasion preparation became the target for American planes which, by that time, would have gained undisputed supremacy in the air. Therefore, the Japanese would have to establish strong defensive positions inland, where they hoped that they could meet and defeat the invaders. To maintain the morale of Thirty-second Army troops at a high level, Ushijima's staff devised the following battle slogan:

One Plane for One Warship

One Boat for One Ship
One Man for Ten of the Enemy
Or One Tank

The strength of the Thirty-second Army and the nature of the terrain of the island it was to defend primarily governed Ushijima's decisions as he prepared his final defense plan. To deceive American assault forces of his intentions, Ushijima's troops were warned 'to guard against opening fire prematurely.' Japanese documents captured by Tenth Army troops after the opening of the campaign disclosed that, rather than forcing the issue on the beaches, 'the Japanese soldier would dig and construct in a way and to an extent that an American soldier has never been known to do.' General Cho was a strong advocate of underground and cave fortifications, and took an active part in setting up his army's defense. Because of its physical characteristics, Okinawa favored the defenders, and the most favorable terrain was occupied and honeycombed with mutually supporting gun positions and covered connecting tunnels. Natural and man-made barriers were effectively in-

corporated to channel attackers into prepared fire lanes and preregistered impact areas. Reverse as well as forward slopes of hills were fortified, while artillery, mortars, and automatic weapons were emplaced in cave mouths and their employment completely integrated into the final protective fire plan.

Unit commanders, from brigade down to company level, were made responsible for organizing the defense and fortification of the sectors assigned to them. In several cases, the requirement for heavy construction in an area was lessened to a great degree by the abundance of large caves which, with but slight reinforcement, could withstand the heaviest bombardments. After these positions were improved, the resulting strongholds were used either as hospitals, barracks, or command posts – or all of these together. When the size of the caves permitted, they were given two or more entrances, and when time and available manpower allowed, more than one level was developed. Tunnels were built leading to automatic weapons and light

artillery positions, which, together with the pillboxes and trenches in the area, dominated each defense sector. Invariably, the approaches and entryways to each cave were guarded by machine guns and, in addition, covering fire from positions outside the caves. These cave strongholds were then integrated within the whole Thirty-second Army defensive system while at the same time serving as the centers of small unit positions. All in all, they formed a vital link in the chain of the tough outer defenses protecting Shuri, where the Thirty-second Army CP was located.

Based on an IGHQ regulation issued to Japanese combat garrisons stating that an 'island must be divided into sectors according to the defense plan so that command will be simplified', each combat organization joining the Thirty-second Army was assigned a sector on Okinawa to develop and defend. The transfer of the 9th Division from Okinawa, however, forced Ushijima to reorganize his defensive alignments.

In developing a final defense plan, Ushijima and his staff were faced with a number of options, each limited by the strength of the Thirty-second Army and its attachments, the nature of the terrain, the overall mission of the Okinawa garrison, and an estimate of American intentions. After considerable study, the Thirty-second Army established a main defense zone along a line north of Naha, Yonabaru, and Shuri. Landings north of this line were to be unopposed, while south of this zone, the invaders would be met at the beaches. Since Ushijima did not have enough troops available to defend Kadena airfield, his 15cm guns would be registered to deny use of the airbase. Although he recognized that his soldiers had not been trained to fight a delaying action, which would prolong the battle, bloody the enemy, and permit the bulk of his Thirty-second Army to withdraw to the more defensible southern portion of Okinawa, this, nevertheless, was the strategy he was forced to adopt after the initial American landings.

The main Japanese battle position was established in the Shuri area, where the rugged terrain surrounding the ancient capital of the Okinawan kings was developed with the strongest installations oriented to the northwest, toward the Hagushi beaches. Unable to make an accurate estimate regarding American intentions and where they would land, Ushijima guessed that the major enemy assault effort would be in the southeastern portion of the island, across the Minatoga beaches. His decision to defend here was somewhat ironic, for the Iceberg planners had designated the Minatoga beaches an alternate landing area, while the Hagushi beaches were their first choice. The heights of Chinen Peninsula on the east coast dominated both the beaches of Minatoga and Nakagusuku Wan below, and afforded the Japanese the most favorable terrain of its type on Okinawa. Therefore, the greatest proportion of Thirty-second Army artillery and infantry strength was deployed here, rather than in the Shuri area. As a result, the forces diverted to Chinen Peninsula remained there, ineffective for the first few weeks of the fighting.

Shortly after an army-wide reorganization in February 1945, the Thirty-second Army was reorganized once more in March, and its various shipping, air, and rear echelon forces were directed to 'set up organizations and dispositions for land combat.' Besides their normal functions, these units now had to undergo infantry training and at the same time construct their own field fortifications.

At the time of the February reorganization, Thirty-second Army troops were deployed in their final battle positions, awaiting an invasion that was believed not too far distant. The main battle force was established in an outpost zone just north of Futema, while elements of the 1st Specially Established Regiment, under operational control of the 62nd Division, were loosely dispersed in the area immediately behind the Hagushi beaches. Although this was the place where the Americans were considered least likely to land, Ushijima ordered the unit defending this sector to fight a delaying action if the island was invaded here, and then after destroying Yontan and Kadena airfields, to withdraw to the Shuri line. Defending the southernmost portion of Okinawa was the 24th Division and some rear echelon organizations assigned to it. The Okinawa Naval Base Force was charged with the defense of Oroku Peninsula. Here, Admiral Ota's 13mm and 25mm anti-aircraft batteries were re-equipped and transformed into an 81mm mortar battery and two independent machine gun battalions. Thus armed, they were the only adequately weaponed units in the naval garrison.

The bulk of the army's infantry and artillery force was positioned to oppose the landings over the Minatoga beaches. The 5th Artillery Command's CP was established near Itokazu, in direct control of all of its major components, which had been emplaced in defense of the entire

Minatoga region.

Since the center of the Japanese defensive system was located at Shuri, the most valuable and only battle-tested organization on the island, the 62nd Division, was charged with the protection of this vital area. At Shuri, the Japanese had shrewdly and industriously constructed a stronghold centered inside a series of ever-diminishing concentric rings, each of which bristled with well dug-in, expertly sited weapons. Regardless of where the American landings were made, Japanese plans called for delaying actions, and, finally, an orderly withdrawal into the hard shell of these well-organized positions.

The defense of the isolated area north of Ishikawa Isthmus was given over to the Udo Force, so-called after the commander of the 2nd Infantry Unit, Colonel Takehiko Udo. It had a dual mission – defense of both the Motobu Peninsula and of Ie Shima. A reinforced battalion on Ie Shima was assigned a secondary mission of destroying the island's airfield and assisting in the transfer of aviation material to Okinawa. Upon completion of these assignments, it would withdraw to the main island and join the 62nd Division. Udo's second battalion on Motobu, in anticipation of an invasion of Ie Shima followed by a landing on the peninsula, was disposed with its few artillery pieces emplaced to make its position and

Ample sniper cover was to make capturing villages slow and hazardous

positions on Ie Shima mutually supporting. Nonetheless, detached as it was from the bulk of the Thirty-second Army and separated by a considerable distance, Udo's force was consigned to the fate of a forlorn hope.

Ushijima neither planned for an air defense of Okinawa, nor was he given the planes with which to conduct one. Although he had expected that some 300 planes would be sent to the island in April, he knew that their projected date of arrival was too late to influence his situation. Besides, American air and naval bombardments in March 1945, and the preplanned destruction of the Oroku, Kadena, Yontan, and Ie Shima airstrips would prevent their use in any case.

The significance of the Thirty-second Army reorganizations, redeployments, frenzied last-minute preparations, and a general air of expectancy were not lost upon even the rear ranks of the army. One soldier wrote in his diary. 'It's like a frog meeting a snake, and waiting for the snake to eat him.'

Between 20th and 23rd March 1945, the Japanese command on Okinawa made an even more realistic appraisal of what the future held than had the troops. Japanese reaction to news of a meeting in early March of Admirals King and Nimitz in Washington resulted in the establishment of a general alert for the end of March and early April on Okinawa, for statistics revealed 'that new operations occur from twenty days to one month after American conferences on strategy are held.' This Japanese estimate, in addition to increased American air activity over Okinawa and bombardment of the Island as well as reports of increased American shipping in the Marianas and repeated submarine sightings and contacts, enabled the enemy to predict without hesitation that the target was to be 'Formosa or the Nansei Shoto, especially Okinawa.'

Top: Ie Shima airfield, plowed up by the retreating Japanese. *Right:* Typical Okinawan tombs, used by the Japanese as pill boxes, and consequently heavily damaged by US fire

Allied plans and preparations

On 25th October 1944, three weeks following receipt of the JCS directive ordering the Okinawa operation, Nimitz' CinCPOA headquarters published and distributed the Iceberg Joint Staff Study. According to this document, the campaign was to be conducted in three phases, the first of which would see the capture of the southern portion of Okinawa and adjacent small islands. At the same time, units assigned to the Iceberg force for this purpose would begin initial base development in order to transform Okinawa into a massive staging base for further operations against Japan. In Phase II, Ie Shima and the remainder of Okinawa were to be seized and the build-up of the island as a base continued. Allied positions in the Nansei Shoto were to be exploited in Phase III, and when ordered by Nimitz, other islands in the Ryukyus would be captured with forces then available.

The Joint Chiefs of Staff had assembled one of the greatest naval armadas in history for Operation Iceberg. This surface force would transport to the very threshold of Japan 182,000 assault troops – 75,000 more than were landed on D-Day at Normandy. In Spruance's 5th Fleet were more than forty carriers, eighteen battleships, 200 destroyers, and hundreds of other assorted ships of the line, transports, submarines, minesweepers, gunboats, landing ships and craft, and various auxiliary and repair vessels. Assigned to Task Force 51 (Joint Expeditionary Force) alone were 1,213 ships. All told, before the island was secured, about 548,000 Army, Navy, and Marine Corps personnel together with 318 combatant vessels and 1,139 auxiliary vessels exclusive of personnel landing craft of all types were involved in the Okinawa operation.

Strategic commander for Iceberg was Nimitz, while Spruance, whose 5th Fleet and Central Pacific Task Force comprising Task Force 50, was charged with the conduct of the Ryukyus operation itself. In the 5th Fleet were the covering forces and special groups, including the Fast Carrier Force (TF 58) commanded by Vice-Admiral Marc A 'Pete' Mitscher and the British Carrier Force (TF 57)

commanded by Vice-Admiral Sir H Bernard Rawlings, RN. These two forces were scheduled to conduct air strikes prior to the Okinawa landing to neutralize Japanese air power and prevent enemy air and surface elements from interfering with the amphibious assault and the subsequent operations ashore. Also slated to assist the Iceberg effort both prior to and during the course of the campaign were Army Air Forces planes, which would take off from bases in China and the Southwest Pacific.

Most directly concerned with the landing were the components of Admiral Turner's Task Force 51. The complex composition of this force reflected its many assignments incident to the capture, occupation, and defense of Okinawa. Any Japanese attempt to disrupt American movement to or landing operations at the target would be handled by the force's support elements. Other elements would undertake mine-sweeping operations prior to the assault and still others would conduct air support missions and provide air defense of the Tenth Army once the beachhead had been gained. Assigned to these tasks were Rear-Admiral William H P Blandy's Amphibious Support Force (TF 52) and Rear-Admiral Morton L Deyo's Gunfire and Covering Force (TF 54).

In the Northern Attack Force (TF 53) under Rear-Admiral Lawrence R Reifsnider was an assault force comprised of Major General Roy S Geiger's Marine III Amphibious Corps (IIIAC) with the 1st and 6th Marine Divisions under Major-Generals Pedro A del Valle and Lemuel C Shepherd, Jr, respectively. The Southern Attack Force under Rear-Admiral John L Hall, Jr, contained the transports which were to lift the Army assault troops in Major-General John R Hodges' XXIV Corps, comprised of the 7th Infantry Division (Major-General Archibald V Arnold, USA) and the 96th Infantry Division (Major-General James L Bradley, USA).

Three other groups were also part of the Iceberg invasion force – the Western Islands Attack Group (TG 51.1) under Rear-Admiral Ingolf N Kiland, whose assault force was Major-General Andrew D Bruce's 77th Infantry Division; Rear-Admiral Jerauld Wright's Demonstration Group (TG 51.2) and its landing force, Major-General Thomas E Watson's 2nd Marine Division; and the Floating Reserve Group (TG 51.3), commanded by Commodore J B McGovern, carrying the 27th Infantry Division under Major-General George W Griner, Jr, USA.

In addition to IIIAC, one other Marine element for Iceberg was Major-General Francis P Mulcahy's joint air task command, Tactical Air Force, Tenth Army, which was to provide land-based air support for the operation once its squadrons were ashore. The pilots and planes initially assigned to TAF came from the 2nd Marine Aircraft Wing.

A most important segment of TAF was its fighter arm, the Air Defense Command, under Brigadier-General William J Wallace, USMC, whose organization consisted of a headquarters squadron, a service squadron, three Marine aircraft groups with a total complement of nine fighter, two night fighter, and four air warning squadrons. The radar installations of the latter were to become heavily engaged in providing early warning of enemy air attacks within a very short time after the initial landings. An Army Air Force fighter wing was also assigned to the Air Defense Command, but only one of its air groups joined TAF before the Okinawa operation ended.

Army Air Forces flight and support elements made up the whole of General Mulcahy's Bomber Command, but none of these units arrived on Okinawa before the beginning of June. Also part of the TAF organization was an AAF photo-reconnaissance squadron, whose mission was to conduct aerial photographic surveys of enemy installations, interpret the photos it subsequently obtained, and make an aerial survey of the island so that an accurate map of Okinawa could be printed and distributed later.

Rounding out the TAF organization were two Marine torpedo bomber squadrons, which were to conduct anti-submarine operations at the target area in company with carrier-based aircraft. The Marine squadrons

were also directed to be prepared to conduct close support and other missions as ordered.

Marine observation squadrons, which were not organic to TAF, were also to play an important role in the operation, for their artillery spotting capability while attached to the Marine divisions as well as the two corps of the Tenth Army provided a useful service to the ground forces. Rounding out the air elements of the Tenth Army were the Landing Force Air Support Control Units, the LFASCUs, under Colonel Vernon E Megee, a veteran Marine aviator like Generals Geiger, Mulcahy, and Wallace. The LFASCUs were to control all air support of the infantry forces, and when so directed by Admiral Turner, they would set up ashore at the headquarters of the Tenth Army and the two corps also. At this time, responsibility for air control operations would be transfered from the Navy shipboard unit to the Marines on Okinawa.

General Buckner was not only responsible for the assault and consolidation phases of Iceberg, but he

An amtrack carries Major-General Archibald V Arnold ashore

was also concerned with the garrison phase. His Island Commander was Major-General Fred C Wallace, USA, whose command would include the Ie Shima Garrison and, on Okinawa, the Naval Operating Base and the Naval Air Bases, once they were established ashore. Upon completion of the amphibious phase of Iceberg, Rear-Admiral Calvin H Cobb would assume command of the Naval Forces, Ryukyus. While strategic air force and naval search squadrons were to be based on Okinawa, they would remain under the operational control of the Commanding General, Army Air Forces, Pacific Ocean Areas, and the Commander, Fifth Fleet, respectively.

The tasks assigned to this formidable expeditionary force and its naval support evolved from the tactical concepts underlying the Okinawa assault as stated in the Iceberg Joint Staff Study and later incorporated in the TF 50 operation plan. This plan was also based on Admiral Turner's estimate of the situation, in which he

assumed that Japanese air would bitterly react to the American landing; that enemy submarines would be active in the target area; that the Japanese fleet might sortie out from bases in the Home Islands to attack the invasion flotilla; and that the enemy might attempt to reinforce the Okinawa garrison. Of these four assumptions, the first three were proved valid. The fourth was not tested because, in accordance with the provisions of the JCS directive unleashing Iceberg, Allied air and surface supremacy had to be and were gained in the target area prior to L-Day, as the date for the invasion of Okinawa was designated. The assumption which bore bitter fruit for the Americans was the first, for Japanese planes and pilots were to maul the naval forces severely at Okinawa.

Governed by Turner's operation plan, the Tenth Army joint staff drew up Plan Fox, which called for an assault landing on the west coast beaches north and south of Hagushi, determined to be the ones best suited for supporting the Iceberg landing. Plan Fox also provided for a pre-L-Day landing on Keise Shima, as a study of this enlarged sand spit showed it could be employed as a fixed emplacement for large-caliber artillery support of the L-Day amphibious assault.

When Buckner's Tenth Army plan was presented on 1st November to Turner and his staff for final approval, the navy in turn argued against certain provisions of the plan. As a result, a revised plan included the capture of Keise Shima and the Kerama Retto prior to the main landing on Okinawa. In particular, seizure of the Keramas was a must for the navy, because this island group could provide a protected anchorage where the supporting naval elements could be refueled and resupplied. Otherwise, they would be forced to conduct their logistical operations in the dangerous and open roadstead off the Hagushi beaches. A small boat pool and seaplane base could also be established in the Kerama anchorage, and they were later.

Rocket bombardment. Part of the pre-invasion softening-up process

The Kerama assault was now a full-sized invasion instead of a raid, as originally envisioned, and as a result, the 2nd Marine Division was assigned this mission. Originally designated IIIAC reserve, Major-General Watson's division had been slated for early commitment in support of operations on Okinawa, and so the 77th Infantry Division (Reinforced) was chosen instead. The 2nd Division was then given the job of conducting a feint landing off the southeastern coast of Okinawa, in the Minatoga region.

As the Iceberg plan expanded in scope and form, Buckner was forced to seek from CinCPOA release of the area reserve unit, the 27th Infantry Division, which was redesignated Tenth Army floating reserve. It was replaced by the 81st Infantry Division, which remained in New Caledonia under direct control of Nimitz.

Plan Baker, the alternate plan for the Iceberg operation, envisioned first the capture of the Kerama Retto and then a sweep of the Eastern Islands by the 2nd Marine Division – both assaults to precede the main landing on Okinawa. On L-Day, IIIAC divisions would establish a beachhead in the area between Chinen Point and Minatoga, secure the high ground, and, following an Army landing two days later, effect a junction with XXIV Corps at Yonabaru. Then, both corps together would drive across the island as rapidly as possible to capture the airfields in their respective zones. Other provisions of the alternate plan called for the capture of Ie Shima, feints against the Chimu Wan area on L plus three or four, and the commitment of Army reserves in either of the corps zones or on the northern flank of XXIV Corps.

Although the approach to the east coast of Okinawa would be more direct than that to the west coast, and the weather on the Pacific side of Okinawa was better than that on the East China Sea coast of the island, the disadvantages of Plan Baker outweighed the advantages. For one thing, the Minatoga beaches were not so good or wide as those in the Hagushi area, and a landing on the east coast would mean that the vital west coast airfields would not be captured as early as desired. Also,

instead of a mass Tenth Army landing over the Hagushi beaches, the invasion effort would be split with two separate corps-sized landings on the east coast. As a result, Plan Fox became the accepted and preferred plan.

The Iceberg scheme of maneuver ashore was designed to secure early use of Kadena and Yontan airfields in order to permit land-based aircraft to gain early supremacy over the target area as well as to acquire bases from which devastating mass air raids could be mounted against Japan. In addition early capture of the airfields meant that air support of the ground forces could begin shortly after the landings.

The 77th Infantry Division was to open on the Iceberg operation by landings on the Kerama Retto on 26th March 1945, six days before L-Day. On 19th November 1944, anticipating bad weather at the target, the original L-Day – 1st March – was pushed forward two weeks to the 15th. This date was again advanced two weeks to 1st April by Nimitz in December, when it appeared doubtful that the shipping assigned to MacArthur's Lingayen Gulf operation could be reassigned

and available in time for employment at Iceberg. So, 1st April, April Fool's Day, and coincidentally Easter Sunday in 1945, was the date finally designated for the invasion of Okinawa.

Following the first day of 77th Division operations in Kerama Retto, and beginning the night of the 26th, Marines of the Amphibious Reconnaissance Battalion, Fleet Marine Force, Pacific (FMFPac), were to reconnoiter the reef islets of the island group. Assigned to support the Hagushi landing, the 420th Field Artillery Group of XXIV Corps would land on Keise Shima with its 15mm guns. Once emplaced, these Long Toms would join in the air and naval gunfire preparation which was to increase in intensity against Okinawa until the assault waves hit the beaches, and then the fire would lift from the beach area and head inland.

With the mouth of the Bishi Gawa marking the initial point of the corps boundary, IIIAC would land on the left and XXIV Corps on the right. Once landed north of Hagushi town, the Marine divisions were to move inland rapidly, pacing their advance with that of the Army corps. On the Marine left flank was the 6th Division; the 22nd Marines on the left and the 4th Marines, less its 2nd Battalion in division reserve, on the right. The 29th Marines, Major-General Shepherd's third rifle regiment, was to be corps reserve, ready to land on any beach on order. His initial mission was the capture of Yontan airfield and the security of the Tenth Army's northernmost flank.

Major-General del Valle's 1st Marine Division, landing on the IIIAC right flank, was to assist in the capture of Yontan by quickly seizing the high ground northeast of the small village of China. His division's axis of attack was straight across the island in pace with the Army units on his right, and then the 1st Division was to drive down the Katchin Peninsula on the east coast. In the 1st Division zone, the 5th and 7th Marines were to be in the assault – 7th on the left – and the 1st Marines in division reserve.

Naval bombardment keeps the enemy's attention while the troops make for the beaches

Left to right: Major George C Axell Jr,
General Alexander A Vandergrift,
Major-General Francis P Mulcahy,
Major Jefferson Dorrah, Lieutenant
Jeremiah J O'Keefe

On the right of the 1st Division
would be Major-General Arnold's 7th
Infantry Division, with the 17th
Infantry on the left, the 32nd Infantry
on the right, and the 184th Infantry in
division reserve. Major-General Bradley's 96th Infantry Division was on
the corps right flank with the 381st
Infantry on the left, 383rd Infantry on
the extreme right flank of the 'Tenth
Army, and the 382nd Infantry assigned
as Major-General Hodges' corps reserve. The 7th Division was to seize
Kadena airfield and then, like the 1st
Division, to advance quickly to the
east coast to cut the island in two.
The 96th was initially required to
capture the high ground commanding
its beaches on the south and southeast, then it was to move down the
coastal road, capture the bridges near
Chatan, all the while guarding the
right flank of the Army from attack
in that quarter.

In addition to organic division

artillery, Marine artillery support
would come from IIIAC Corps Artillery
units, which would land on Geiger's
order. Once ashore, Brigadier-General
David I Nimmer, IIIAC Corps Artillery
commander, would coordinate all
supporting arms operations in the
Marine zone. Less the group on
Keise, Hodges' Corps Artillery, under
Brigadier-General Josef R Sheetz,
would land on order like the Marines,
and support the Army attack.

The operations ashore following
the assault landing were designed to
isolate the Phase I objective, which
comprised that portion of Okinawa
lying south of a general line drawn
across the Ishikawa Isthmus through
China village, and including the
Eastern Islands. To prevent the
enemy from reinforcing from the
north and to fulfill their mission
otherwise in the north, the Marines
were to gain immediate control of
the isthmus. In order to seal off the
Japanese in the south, Army troops
were to sever the island by driving
across Okinawa to its Pacific coast,
with the right flank units manning a
line running through Futema to
Kuba. Once the central portion of

the island had been secured, XXIV Corps divisions would face to the south and continue the attack when all Phase I objectives had been gained.

Iceberg's Phase II consisted of the seizure of northern Okinawa and the capture of Ie Shima by Tenth Army troops locally available after Buckner had determined that Phase I had ended with all missions fulfilled. The primary objective in the north was Motobu Peninsula, which jutted out into the East China Sea and pointed directly at Ie Shima. The peninsula was scheduled to be taken by simultaneously launched attacks from both sea and land. Following capture of Motobu, a shore-to-shore operation would be directed against Ie Shima. Phase II would end with the capture of the rest of northern Okinawa.

Rear-Admiral Calvin T Durgin's carrier-based planes in the TF 52 escort carrier group were slated to handle initial air support of the invasion force. Once Mulcahy's squadrons were ashore and operating, TAF would assume responsibility for overall air defense. As soon as Air Defense Command fighter planes were established on the captured airfields, they would perform their assigned mission of air defense of ground and naval forces by means of combat air patrols, close air support, and other related flight operations.

Because the shipping and troops assigned to Iceberg were dispersed all over the Pacific, the Tenth Army could not train or conduct rehearsals as a cohesive unit. Therefore, the corps and division commanders were made responsible for preparing their own troops for the Okinawa operation along the lines of Tenth Army training directives. The Marine units committed to the Ryukyus assault trained under FMFPac supervision.

The assault forces assigned to Iceberg were, for the most part, veterans of the Pacific fighting. While the Tenth Army, as such, had never directed any combat operation before this, its corps and divisions had all been combat-tested before the Okinawa landing. XXIV Corps had carried out the conquest of Leyte, and was, in fact, deeply involved in the Philippines campaign and not released to the Tenth Army by Mac-

Arthur until 10th February 1945, almost two months before L-Day. The 7th Infantry Division had participated in the Attu, Kwajalein, and Leyte operations; the 77th Division had been blooded on Guam and Leyte; and the 96th Division – originally scheduled to make the Yap landing, which was later cancelled – first fought on Leyte. The 27th Division had taken part in the battles for the Gilberts and Marshalls and had also landed on Saipan.

Geiger's III Amphibious Corps had captured Guam and Peleliu, while its predecessor command, I Marine Amphibious Corps had achieved an outstanding record in the battles leading to the capture of the entire Solomons chain. The 1st Marine Division had made the first American assault landing in the Pacific War on Guadalcanal and had also made the amphibious assault landings against the Japanese on New Britain at Cape Gloucester, and at Peleliu, a little-heralded but bloody fight in the Palaus. The ranks of the 1st Division held 5,846 officers and enlisted Marines who had served overseas nearly thirty months by 1945, and who had participated in the division's three campaigns; a number of these men were to fight on Okinawa also.

Similarly, the ranks of the 6th Marine Division, activated on Guadalcanal in September 1944, held veterans of other Marine campaigns in the Pacific. The division was formed around the 1st Provisional Marine Brigade, which had landed on Guam with the 4th and 22nd Marines. The 4th Marines was composed of the disbanded Marine Raider battalions which had fought on Guadalcanal, New Georgia, and Bougainville. This was the 'New' 4th Marines, which took on the title and was to carry on the traditions of the 'Old' 4th Marines, captured *in toto* at the time that Corregidor fell in 1942.

After its reactivation the 4th, as a whole, had landed on Emirau and Guam. The 22nd Marines had taken part in the Eniwetok and Guam operations, while the 1st Battalion, 29th Marines (1/29) had reinforced the 2nd Marine Division for the Saipan assault. Following its relief on Saipan, the battalion was sent to Guadalcanal, where it awaited the arrival of its two sister battalions from the States and eventual assignment to the 6th Division. Most of the men in the division had fought in at least one campaign – Guam – and many were now beginning a second tour of overseas combat duty. The 2nd Marine Division was a veteran of the Guadalcanal, Tarawa, Saipan, and Tinian operations. Its troops, like those in the other Marine divisions, were veterans and experts in the conduct of amphibious assault operations, a technique which the Marine Corps had developed to a high degree of perfection in the prewar years.

Although the major assault components of the Tenth Army were battle experienced for the most part, they still needed to conduct extensive training programs in order to bring veteran and newly joined replacements alike to peak fighting trim. On-the-job training was conducted by XXIV Corps units involved in the late stages of mopping-up operations on Leyte. In like manner, the 2nd Marine Division on Saipan effectively integrated a division-wide training program into their mopping-up operations against enemy holdouts on the island.

The 6th Marine Division trained on Guadalcanal, its base, while the 1st Marine Division conducted small-unit training problems on Pavuvu, its island base in the Russells, some sixty-five miles northwest of Guadalcanal. When the training cycle of the division reached the regimental level and outgrew Pavuvu's meagre facilities, each regimental combat team – an infantry regiment reinforced with supporting elements – was rotated to Guadalcanal for a period of approximately two weeks of intensive combined arms training. All 1st Division artillery firing problems had to be conducted on Guadalcanal because of the lack of suitable firing ranges in the Russells.

The 27th Infantry Division, the most isolated Tenth Army unit, arrived on Espiritu Santo, New Hebrides, from Saipan in October 1944, when it, too, began an intensive training cycle. The division was undivided in its low opinion of Espiritu

Santo as a poor rehabilitation and training base because of the island's torrid climate, poor topography, and lush, tropic jungles.

While the assault divisions were busily engaged in training for Okinawa, Buckner's staff was deeply involved in administative and logisitical preparations for Okinawa. Fortunately, most of the planning already accomplished for the cancelled Formosan venture could be salvaged with but few changes for Iceberg. The logistics plan for Okinawa was 'the most elaborate one of its kind developed during the Second World War, involving prearranged movement of both assault and cargo shipping over vast ocean distances.' The plan, as it evolved, called for the establishment of a 6,000-mile-long supply line stretched across the Pacific, with eleven different ports-

of-call, to support the mounting of 182,821 troops encumbered with 746,850 measurement tons of cargo loaded into 434 assault transports and landing ships.

Each Service was responsible for initially supporting its own units in the Okinawa task force. The only exceptions were the troops mounting at South and Southwest Pacific bases. Commanders in these theaters were charged with logistical support of Iceberg troops. After L-Day and when the troops were ashore – and

Boeing B-29 Superfortress

when directed by Turner – Tenth Army's Island Command would take over as Buckner's central support agency charged with furnishing supplies to all of the assault forces. As the Iceberg operation unfolded and Tenth Army needs developed, the magnitude of the overall logistics required to support Iceberg became apparent. The comparison of Iceberg with other Pacific operations may be seen in the table:

Operation	Number of Ships	Personnel	Measurement Tons
Gilberts	63	35,214	148,782
Marshalls	122	85,201	293,792
Marianas	210	141,519	437,753
Leyte	110	57,411	214,552
Palaus	109	55,887	199,963
Iwo Jima	174	86,516	180,447
Okinawa	434	182,821	746,850

In addition to its other functions, Tenth Army Island Command was also responsible for the establishment of military government operations on Okinawa. Since this was the first Pacific operation in which large numbers of enemy civilians were to be encountered, it was anticipated that Okinawa would serve as a valuable testing ground for civil affairs and military government practices which could be employed when Japan itself was occupied. The Chief Military Government Officer was made directly subordinate to the Island Commander and was, in fact, designated his deputy. This close relationship was justified as the campaign progressed. By 30th April, there were approximately 125,000 Okinawans under civil jurisdiction. This figure climbed steadily from this time, for it reached 147,820 by 31st May, 172,670 by 15th June, and totaled 261,115 on 30th June.

Equally as busy as the logistics staff were the intelligence planners,

Typical of the difficult terrain revealed by later reconnaissance

although they had much less firm information to work with. Current intelligence was hard to come by because of Okinawa's location within the Empire's well-protected inner defenses. For the most part, documents and prisoners captured elsewhere, as well as former inhabitants of the island – many of whom were plantation workers in the Hawaiian Islands – and old Japanese publications provided the basis on which intelligence of Okinawa was produced. In addition, Turner's staff discovered that living in the United States was an American who had spent many years in Japan and Okinawa. He was immediately pressed into service as a source of much valuable information.

The first aerial photographic mission over Okinawa was flown in September 1944 by B-29s. Unfortunately, the results of this mission were poor because of the heavy cloud cover which generally existed over most of the island. As a result of this inadequate coverage, the first maps produced from these photos had many blank spaces and were not

revised until the middle of the operation. Captured enemy maps produced more thorough terrain information. Additional aerial photos were obtained during the fast carrier raids beginning 10th October 1944. From the B-29 flight in September to 28th March 1945, a total of 224 photo-reconnaissance missions were flown over the target and much valuable intelligence derived as a result. In addition, target information lists were compiled, constantly revised, and distributed to artillery, air, and naval gunfire agencies. To supplement the aerial photograph, USS *Swordfish*, a specially equipped submarine, was sent to Okinawa from Pearl Harbor on 22nd December 1944 with the mission of photographing Japanese beach and coastal defenses. The sub's last-known transmission was received on 3rd January 1945. She was never heard from again, and was later listed as missing in action.

From the time that the Okinawa invasion was ordered in October 1944 until the very end of the campaign, Tenth Army order of battle lists constantly revised enemy strength figures. Originally, Japanese strength on Okinawa was estimated at 48,600 men. In January 1945, this figure was revised upwards to 66,000, and it was assumed that if the enemy exerted his maximum reinforcement capability, total strength could amount to 87,000 troops. In all truth, the Tenth Army was never able to arrive at a firm enemy troop estimate. The G-2 agencies were a bit more accurate in determining possible enemy courses of action, for these were analyzed in light of what was then known of current Japanese tactical doctrine. All indications pointed to the fact that the enemy would organize the southern third of Okinawa for a defense in depth, while the bulk of Thirty-second Army troops would be held as mobile reserve. If this was to be the case on L-Day, then the assault forces faced a potentially more dangerous situation than if they were to meet the more commonly experienced Japanese tactic of a determined beach defense.

Air and naval capabilities attributed to the enemy remained relatively unchanged during the pre-L-Day period. At all times, it was anticipated that the Japanese were capable of mounting heavy and repeated air attacks against invasion shipping. It was also anticipated that the Japanese suicide air tactics first unleashed during the Leyte operation would be repeated and increasingly intensified at Okinawa. Estimated enemy air strength within striking range was placed at 3,000 planes. Along with this air capability was the enemy's ability to mount an airborne counterattack, for if the enemy was to become truly desperate, this was, in fact, the only way in which he could reinforce his Okinawa garrison.

While the Japanese navy was no longer strong, it still retained powerful enough operational forces within range of Okinawa, and these posed a threat to the Iceberg invasion force. It was definitely known however, that the Japanese had suicide motor torpedo boat squadrons at Okinawa, and the possibility existed that midget submarines were based there, also. In addition to the potential threat offered by these suicide units was the possible employment of suicide swimmers, whose task, also, was destruction of invasion shipping in the anchorages off target area beaches. As it transpired, the major threat to Iceberg was not to come from the sea.

The proximity of Leyte to Okinawa permitted XXIV Corps to mount and stage in that area, although a portion of Southern Attack Force shipping was to load Tenth Army and Island Command troops at Oahu as well. Destined to open the Okinawa operation with a landing in the Kerama Retto, the 77th Infantry Division left from Leyte on 19th and 21st March. The Southern Tractor Flotilla, carrying the 7th and 96th Divisions departed Leyte in the morning hours of 24th March, and the transport groups left three days later.

The Northern Attack Force embarked IIIAC divisions at Guadalcanal and Pavuvu, and picked up some TAF tactical squadrons at Espiritu Santo. On 12th March, the Northern Tractor Flotilla was the first increment of TF 53 to depart

The suicide planes strike.
Above: Damage to USS *Hancock*
Left: A near miss for USS *Cabot*

the Solomons for the rendezvous area at Ulithi. To avoid subjecting the troops to a long and debilitating sea voyage under crowded conditions, they were loaded aboard transports for the first stage of the trip and would transfer to LSTs and LSMs at Ulithi. Northern Attack Force transports left the Solomons on 17th March, and six days later both it and the tractor group arrived at Ulithi, America's westernmost fleet anchorage, staging base, and repair depot in the Pacific. Here, the war was brought home to the men in the Iceberg forces when, in the gloomy, fog-bound Saturday afternoon of 24th March, the battered carrier *Franklin*, escorted by the cruiser *Santa Fe*, limped into the anchorage. The 'Big Ben', as she was familiarly called, had been severely damaged by suicide planes during TF 38 fast carrier strikes against enemy shipping at Kure and Kobe on 19th March, the date of her last combat duty in the war.

On 25th March, the Northern Tractor Flotilla, now with assault troops on board, steamed from Ulithi for Okinawa. Two days later, the remainder of the assault echelon set forth in its wake. On the same dates, the Demonstration Group, with the 2nd Marine Division on board, departed Saipan. Oahu was the scene of the departure of most of the TAF assault echelon, although one Marine aircraft group left from Roi-Namur in the Marshalls and joined the Okinawa-bound shipping which steamed out of Saipan.

Meanwhile, beginning with the fast carrier strikes of 10th October, preliminary carrier strikes and naval gunfire bombardments served to alert the Okinawa garrison that it had, at last, become the focal interest of American intentions. The island was visited for a second time by carrier forces on 3rd and 4th January 1945. One Japanese replacement complained in his diary that 'seeing enemy planes for the first time since coming to Okinawa gave me the feeling of being in a combat zone . . .' Navy planes returned to the island

The 155mm gun (United States)
The most important weapon in the USA's long range artillery inventory, the
155mm gun, nicknamed 'Long Tom', had a specially designed carriage which
enabled it to move across country and could defeat any other piece of
heavy artillery. Its maximum range was 25,715 yards and its rate of fire
one round per minute

on 22nd January and shook his complacency further. That he resented their presence is apparent in his following diary notation: 'While some fly around overhead and strafe, the big bastards fly over the airfield and drop bombs. The ferocity of the bombing is terrific. It really makes me furious. It is past 1500 and the raid is still on. At 1800 the last two planes brought the raid to a close. What the hell kind of bastards are they? Bomb from 0600 to 1800!'

In addition to their strikes on Okinawa, Task Force 38 planes struck Formosa and South China coastal ports, while they covered the Luzon landings in the same period. As a diversion for the Marine assault of Iwo Jima on 19th February, Mitscher's Fast Carrier Force struck the Tokyo area 16th-17th February and 25th February. At the same time that the carrier-based planes were punishing the enemy, American submarines and naval patrol bombers ranged the western Pacific, all the while taking an ever-increasing toll of enemy shipping. By mid-February 1945, the Okinawa garrison was all but isolated. Ushijima was well aware that his command now stood alone, for the line of communication between Formosa and the mainland of Japan had been practically severed.

Okinawa was further neutralized and isolated by a continuous series of air strikes on the Japanese industrial network in the Home Islands by AAF bombers mounting attacks from bases in China, India, the Philippines, the Marianas, and the Palaus. Giant B-29s in ever-increasing numbers also rose from Marianas fields to hit Tokyo, Kobe, Nagoya, and Osaka in devastating fire-bombing raids. Throughout the western Pacific, the tempo of covering operations accelerated with the approach of L-Day. For its final strike against Japan prior to the Okinawa landing, Task Force 58 (whose designation was changed from TF 38 on 27th January when Spruance relieved Admiral William F Halsey, and Mitscher relieved Vice-Admiral John S McCain as head of the Fast Carrier Force) steamed out of Ulithi on 14th March. Four days later, Kyushu was struck, and on the 19th, installations in

Shikoku and Honshu were attacked, but not without damage in return to the American fleet. Five carriers and other shipping in the task force were hurt badly. The remaining ships in TF 58 – the carriers, battleships, and the protective screen – were reorganized on 22nd March into three task groups of relatively equal strength and began their final run on Okinawa for a period of preinvasion bombardments.

The first elements of the Iceberg Force to appear at Okinawa were the doughty minesweepers, which began clearing operations off Kerama Retto and the southeast coast of Okinawa on 24th March, just two days before the 77th Division was scheduled to land. After a channel had been cleared outside the 100 fathom curve off the Minatoga beaches, Mitscher's battleships steamed through the cleared area and began blasting the island while TF 58 planes overhead protected the naval gunfire ships and at the same time neutralized coastal installations by bombing and strafing runs.

While these operations were underway, the Amphibious Support Force (TF 54) had completed its run from Ulithi and had deployed into an approach formation. Two fire support units left the force and began their respective assignments – one to cover the sweeping operations underway between Tonachi Shima and Kerama Retto, and the second to cover the minesweepers off Okinawa and to begin bombarding the demonstration beaches. At the same time, ten underwater demolition teams from the Underwater Demolition Flotilla were organized in Groups Able and Baker on board high-speed destroyer transports. Group Able and destroyers of the Gunfire and Covering Force formed for naval gunfire and UDT operations scheduled for the 25th at Kerama Retto.

As vaster areas surrounding Okinawa were swept clear of mines, destroyers and gunboats increased the isolation of the Okinawa garrison. Disposed at various points from fifteen to one hundred miles off shore, radar picket vessels encircled the island to provide the invasion force with early warning of enemy air raids. Aboard the destroyer and destroyer-minesweeper radar pickets were fighter-director teams which controlled the carrier-plane combat air patrols (CAPs) which orbited overhead during daylight hours. When the pickets' radar screens showed bogies heading their way, the CAPs were vectored out to intercept and destroy the Japanese intruders. The bulk of the very heavy losses sustained by the Navy during the battle for Okinawa was born by vessels of the radar picket fleet – while the remainder of Allied shipping losses resulted from Japanese suicide planes which managed to elude the CAP aircraft. This destruction, rather than the casualties incurred during the ground fighting, threatened the success of the operation overall.

Although American raids on Kyushu had generally disrupted Japanese plans for mounting air attacks from the Home Islands, enemy planes based elsewhere were not so well subdued. As soon as the Japanese perceived that Okinawa was indeed the target and that waters surrounding the island held lucrative targets, elements of the enemy 8th Air Fleet rose from fields on Sakishima Gunto to make the first *Kamikaze* attack at dawn on 26th March on ships standing off the Kerama Retto. As part of its preliminary operations in support of Iceberg, the British Carrier Force had struck the Sakishimas on the 26th and 27th of March. Since Allied carriers thus blocked the use of Kyushu and Sakishima Gunto as bases from which his air attacks could be mounted against the invasion forces, the enemy had to employ his Okinawa-based aircraft instead. In three suicidal forays, all available planes, including trainers, liaison craft, and Special Attack Unit aircraft, which managed to slip in from Kyushu, were expended against the invaders and resulted in the complete elimination of the Okinawa garrison's air strength by 29th March.

While the claims of enemy pilots who managed to return home safely were grossly exaggerated, the destruction they visited upon invasion shipping was extensive. For the period 26th-31st March, a total of six American ships, including Spruance's flagship *Indianapolis*, was struck by Japanese suicide planes. Near misses accounted for damage to ten other vessels, floating mines sank two ships, and a Japanese torpedo boat damaged still another boat.

These efforts were not sufficient to deter Iceberg assault preparations, however. Four Group Able UDTs cleared Kerama beach approaches on 26th March and began blowing Keise Shima reefs the next day. Reconnaissance and demolition work scheduled to begin at Okinawa on the 28th was held up for a day until all minesweeping operations there had been completed. Elements of Group Able worked over the demonstration beaches on the 29th, while at the same time Group Baker teams reconnoitered the Hagushi beaches. The obstacles at Hagushi were negligible, although the teams discovered approximately 2,900 wooden posts embedded in the reef off the Bishi Gawa. On 30th March, they were blown up by hand-placed charges.

The scheduled naval gunfire preparation of Okinawa began on 25th March, and at the same time, carrier-based aircraft pounded the island repeatedly against ineffectual and desultory antiaircraft fire. During the course of 3,095 sorties that the TF 52 Combat Air Support Control Unit directed against Okinawa prior to L-Day, special attention was paid to the destruction of submarine pens, airfields, suicide boat installations, bridges over the roads leading to the landing area, and both covered and uncovered gun positions. Although Rear-Admiral Blandy's force expended 27,226 rounds of 5-inch or heavier caliber ammunition against the target area, extensive damage was caused only to surface installations, and especially those in the vicinity of the airfields. As Tenth Army ground forces discovered later, the enemy sustained little damage to their well dug-in defenses and few casualties amongst the troops who manned them. While Blandy could state on the day before the Okinawa assault that 'the preparation was sufficient for a successful landing', he also admitted that 'we did not conclude from the enemy silence

Above: The ships move up. *Below:* Securing Takashiki Shima in the Kerama Retto

that all defense installations had been destroyed . . .'

The Keramas received an equally intensive air and naval gunfire preparation. Even if Kerama Retto had held no value to the Allies as an advanced logistics base and fleet anchorage, it would have had to be taken because of the threat it offered to the primary invasion effort against Okinawa. Confirmed when the 77th Division landed was the presence in this island group of a suicide sea raiding squadron, for immediately after landing, Army troops discovered and destroyed 350 enemy suicide boats, some of them booby-trapped. According to instructions from higher authority, these small marauders were to speed from their hideouts in the Keramas' small islands to the American anchorage, where 'the objective of the attack will be transports, loaded with essential supplies and material and personnel . . .' Ushijima also ordered such attacks 'carried out by concentrating maximum strength immediately upon the enemy's landing.' Unfortunately for the Japanese, the surprise American thrust into the Keramas frustrated this plan, and undoubtedly assured a successful Hagushi landing, safe, at least, from a waterborne threat. When the 77th Division landed, the Keramas were defended by approximately 975 enemy troops, of which only the nearly 300 suicide boat operators had any combat value. The rest of the garrison was composed of about 600 Korean laborers and nearly one hundred base troops.

At 0801, the 26th of March, the first of the four assault battalions of the 77th Division hit its assigned target and in less than an hour's time, the others had attacked their objectives. Before noon, when Major-General Bruce observed that the rapid progress of his troops ashore would permit yet another landing that day, he ordered the 2nd Battalion, 307th Infantry, a reserve unit, to take Yakabi Shima. The battalion landed against little resistance and secured its objective by 1341. By the end of the day, the Army division had done very well in seizing three islands outright and establishing a firm foothold on two others.

Within the period 26th-31st March, the 77th Infantry Division completely accomplished its mission as the vanguard of the Tenth Army at a cost of thirty-one men killed and another eighty-one wounded. In the course of its operations, the division killed 530 enemy soldiers, captured 121 more, and rounded up some 1,195 civilians. Yet, some Japanese troops remained at large on the islands of the group and were in occasional communication with the Thirty-second Army on Okinawa. It was not too long before these holdouts, too, were either captured or killed.

Marine Corps participation in pre-L-Day activities was undertaken by the FMFPac Amphibious Reconnaissance Battalion attached to the Tenth Army and commanded by Major James L Jones, USMC. On the night of 26th-27th March, while the 77th Division consolidated its day's gains and prepared for further operations, the Marines landed on and reconnoitered the reef islets comprising Keise Shima. After gaining important beach and terrain information, and finding no enemy, the Marines reboarded their high-speed destroyer transports, the APDs. During the next night, the Marine scouts landed on Aware Shima, a small island off the tip of Tokashiki Shima, and in the early morning hours of 29th March, they reconnoitered Mae and Kure Shimas. On 31st March, the 155mm Long Toms of the 420th Field Artillery Group landed on Keise Shima and by 1935 that evening, began firing registration on Okinawa.

In contrast to the quite open pre-L-Day operations of the Iceberg forces, the Japanese were able to shroud their tactical dispositions with a greater degree of secrecy. It was not until some time after the initial amphibious assault on Okinawa that Tenth Army troops were able to discover where the Japanese were. This enemy reluctance to tip his hand at an early time combined with Ushijima's intention to defend the southeastern coastal area of Okinawa weighted the scales in favor of an unopposed American landing over the Hagushi beaches.

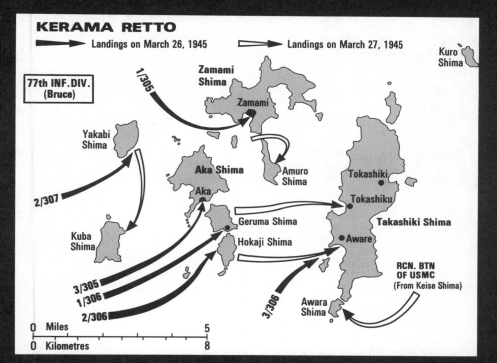

The assault on the Kerama Retto

Assault
on
Okinawa

The morning of Easter Sunday, 1st April 1945, at Okinawa was cloudy with clearing skies. The sea was calm and surf conditions were moderate. Easterly to northeasterly offshore winds carried the smoke of bursting bombs and naval shells away from the beaches, and the seventy-five degree temperature felt comfortably cool to the many veteran jungle fighters in the invasion force. While landing ships and transports took their positions off Hagushi and prepared to disgorge their assault wave troops, amphibian tractors and landing craft, Demonstration Group shipping off Minatoga carried out the same preparations for the feint landings.

With the traditional order, 'Land the landing force', at 0406 Turner unleashed his powerful command against the Japanese defenders of Okinawa. Initial enemy reaction to the invasion occurred shortly after dawn when he sent scattered air attacks against the transport areas. Believing that the major American effort was directed at the Minatoga area, the few Japanese planes not destroyed by combat air patrol aircraft or ships' antiaircraft fire disregarded the targets massed off Hagushi and concentrated on Demonstration Group shipping instead. Suicide planes struck the transport *Hinsdale* and LST 884 as troops were loading into landing craft and amtracs for the feint run into the beaches. As a result of this air attack, eight Marines were killed, thirty-seven wounded, and eight listed as missing in action. It was somewhat ironic that these troops from 3/2 and its reinforcing elements – the first Iceberg casualties on L-Day – were not even scheduled to land.

Air support arrived over the target area at 0650, and debarkation activities began ten minutes later. The Hagushi transport area was a beehive of activity as troops clambered down landing nets into waiting landing craft at the same time that both armored amphibians and amphibian tractors already loaded with troops and equipment spewed from the open jaws of LSTs and tank-laden LCMs floated from flooded well decks of LSDs. Other tanks, equipped with

flotation gear, dropped into the water from open LSTs and prepared to make their own way to the beaches.

As the assault wave began forming for the run to the beachhead, the massed fires of ten battleships, nine cruisers, twenty-three destroyers, and the Long Toms on Keise Shima heralded the approach of the invaders. Against this murderous pounding, the Japanese returned only slight and ineffectual fire, but did manage to deliver heavy enough counterbattery fire against the 420th Field Artillery Group on Keise to hold up unloading

operations on the reef for four hours
without causing damage to either the
guns or the supply buildup. As if
flaunting its power in the face of the
enemy, the assault waves formed up
within sight and range of Japanese
weapons, but neither troops nor
landing craft were hit, though fired
upon.

Control vessels lay off the Okinawa
beaches to mark the lines of departure
for each assault unit. At 0800, after
landing craft and vehicles had formed
into waves behind the LD, the control
vessels hauled down their signal pen-

**Invasion beach panorama. Japanese
tactics have changed, and the landings
meet with little resistance**

nants and the armored LVTs comprising the assault wave raced forward toward the beaches in an almost
unbroken line, eight miles from flank
to flank. Leading the way in were
gunboats firing rockets, mortars, and
40mm guns into prearranged target
squares on such a scale that the
landing area for 1,000 yards inland
was blanketed with enough 5-inch
shells, 4.2-inch mortars, and 4.5-inch

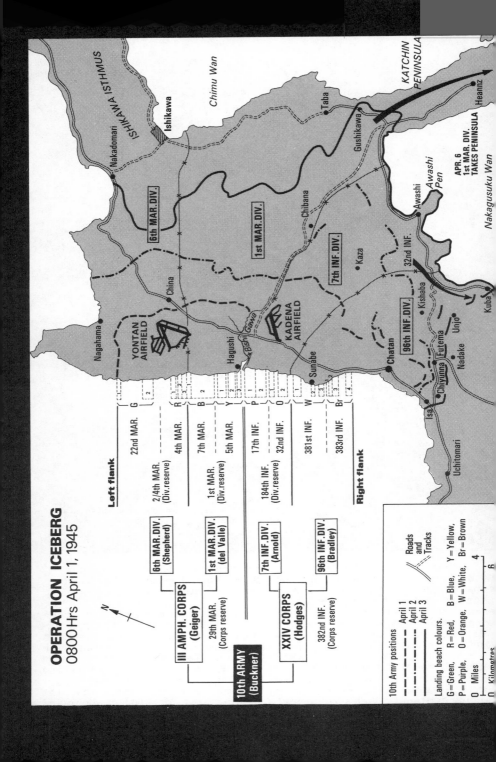

OPERATION ICEBERG
0800 Hrs April 1, 1945

Left flank

10th ARMY (Buckner)

III AMPH. CORPS (Geiger)
- 6th MAR. DIV. (Shepherd)
- 1st MAR. DIV. (del Valle)
- 29th MAR. (Corps reserve)

XXIV CORPS (Hodges)
- 7th INF. DIV. (Arnold)
- 96th INF. DIV. (Bradley)
- 382nd INF. (Corps reserve)

22nd MAR. — G — 2
2/4th MAR. (Div. reserve)
4th MAR. — R — 3
— 2
— 1
B — 2
7th MAR. — Y — 1
1st MAR. (Div. reserve) — 2
5th MAR. — 3
P — 2
17th INF. — 1
184th INF. (Div. reserve) — 2
32nd INF. — O — 2
— 1
W — 3
381st INF. — 2
383rd INF. — Br — 3
— 4

Right flank

10th Army positions
- April 1
- April 2
- April 3

Roads and Tracks

Landing beach colours.
G = Green, R = Red, B = Blue, Y = Yellow,
P = Purple, O = Orange, W = White, Br = Brown

Miles 0 4
Kilometres 0 6

Nagahama
YONTAN AIRFIELD
China
Hagushi
Bishi Gawa
KADENA AIRFIELD
Sunabe
Chatan
Isa
Chiyunna
Uchitomari
Nadake
Unjo
Futema
Kishaba
Kaza
Chibana
Awashi
Awashi Pen
Kuba
Nakagusuku Wan

Nakadomari
Ishikawa
SHIKAWA ISTHMUS
Chimu Wan
Taba
Gushikawa
Heanza
KATCHIN PENINSULA
APR. 6
1st MAR. DIV.
TAKES PENINSULA

6th MAR. DIV.
1st MAR. DIV.
7th INF. DIV.
96th INF. DIV.
32nd INF.

N

rockets to average twenty-five rounds in each one hundred yard square. Upon reaching the reefs, the gunboats and control vessels turned aside and the amtracs passed through them and proceeded the rest of the way to the beaches unescorted. When the gunboats ceased firing, the armored amtracs took over, firing their 75mm howitzers directly ahead of them at targets of opportunity on the beach until the landing. Following on schedule at regular intervals, hundreds of troop-laden LVTs, five to seven waves deep, crossed the line of departure and headed determinedly for the beaches.

As the assault wave approached the end of their 4,000-yard run to the beaches, naval gunfire lifted from the beachhead to hit other targets inland. When the ships' gunfire lifted, carrier planes which had been lazily orbiting overhead began diving on the landing area to neutralize it further with repeated bombing and strafing runs.

By 0830, the first waves began to touch down on their assigned zones. Despite the fringing reef off their beaches and enemy mortar fire seeking their range, the eight XXIV Corps assault battalions, which had been carried ashore in six successive waves of armored LVTs, landed successfully south of the Bishi Gawa. A sea wall, which was of some concern during planning stages of the operation, had been well breached by naval gunfire, and combat engineers assigned to the first waves blasted those sections of the wall still standing to provide additional beach exits. Successive waves of amtracs poured through these new breaches and fanned out to protect the flanks of the infantry, while DUKWs – amphibian trucks – preloaded with 4.2-inch mortars and their crews, and tanks as well, rolled inland to expand the Army beachhead.

North of the Bishi Gawa, IIIAC Marines poured ashore against the same surprising lack of resistance experienced by the soldiers. Before the invasion was an hour old, all assault elements of the 1st and 6th Marine Divisions north of the corps boundary had landed, and south of the Bishi Gawa, XXIV Corps had landed the assault forces of the 7th and 96th Divisions. In an amphibious operation conducted in a classic manner, the Tenth Army had put more than 16,000 combat troops ashore in the first hour of Operation Iceberg.

Wonder of wonders, the entire Okinawa landing had taken place with surprising ease, against little or no enemy gunfire, and no troops, mines, or obstacles on the beaches. More than one combat veteran of other Pacific operations wondered what was in store, what tricks the enemy was reserving for the future, and in what manner the Japanese had baited this trap, for it had to be a trap of some sort. Standing on a hill overlooking the Bishi Gawa, a 7th Division infantryman expressed a feeling common to other Tenth Army soldiers and Marines when he said, 'I've already lived longer than I thought I would.' Once the troops threw off that tense feeling that always accompanied them in an attack, their spirits rose as they looked about them at the dry land, green with conifers and other vegetation so different from the swamps, savannahs, and palm trees they knew in the tropics. Even the air they breathed was cool and bracing. After a quick survey of the land about them, the units went back to the business at hand, formed up, and began an orderly move inland according to plan.

On the southeast coast of Okinawa, meanwhile, Watson's 2nd Division Marines continued their diversionary tactics. Covered by a smoke screen, seven boat waves consisting each of twenty-four loaded landing craft headed for the Minatoga beaches. At 0830 – H-Hour for the Hagushi landings – the fourth wave of the feint landing crossed its line of departure, and then all boats reversed course. By 1500, all boats had been recovered by parent vessels and all troops re-embarked. The only enemy response to the feint, other than the air raid mentioned earlier, was a four-round salvo which found no target. On 2nd April, the feint was repeated, and then all boats and troops again recovered. Demonstration Group shipping then upped their anchors and steamed away from the area.

Ingrained with a caution born out of previous experiences in other en-

The virtually unopposed landings.
Troops and supplies pour ashore on the
beaches and Marines advance inland to
establish positions

The Landing Vehicle, Tracked
In their island hopping campaigns in the Pacific, American forces found that the most difficult part of any assault landing was the first contact with the shore, when Japanese guns in concealed positions could fire on stationary troops in exposed positions. To counter this lack of mobility, the Buffalo (LVT or Landing Vehicle, Tracked) was developed; developed from this again was the LVT(A) (Howitzer) to provide troops on the beaches with some heavy firepower. Specification for LVT(A) (Howitzer): *Weight:* 13.7 tons. *Armament:* one 75mm M-3 howitzer and two .5-inch Browning machine guns. *Maximum speed:* 20 mph on land and 7½ mph in the water

counters with the Japanese, assault troops on the west coast moved up the slightly rising ground raising from the beaches and headed inland. Their immediate objectives were Yontan and Kadena airfields, each about a mile away from the beaches. At about 1000, 7th Division patrols were on Kadena airfield and found it totally deserted; thirty minutes later, the front lines of XXIV Corps were beyond the field. With similar ease, the 4th Marines advanced to Yontan against scattered resistance offered by isolated enemy pockets built around light machine gun nests. Colonel Alan Shapley's Marines found Yontan field deserted also, but its administration buildings were intact and its antiaircraft artillery positions empty and containing only dummy guns. Yontan was declared secured at 1300 and the 4th Marines continued the attack a half-hour later.

The Tenth Army advance generally halted for the day between 1500 and 1600, and the troops prepared night defenses at the furthermost point of the advance. At nightfall, the beachhead was 15,000 yards wide and some 5,000 yards deep. Ashore were more

than 60,000 men including the reserve regiments of both corps. Enemy resistance had been sporadic and desultory. All divisional artillery was ashore and direct support battalions had emplaced, were registered, and were prepared to respond to calls for fire support. A large portion of Tenth Army armor was also ashore, as were 15,000 service troops and some miscellaneous AAA units.

By dark, most of the front line was tied in, and where gaps existed, they were covered by either reserve units or by organic weapons. Primary enemy reaction to the landing was in the form of air attacks which had only limited success. Suicide planes hit Demonstration Group shipping, the *West Virginia*, two transports, and an LST. Several other ships were damaged, but not seriously. An uncounted number of Japanese planes had been shot down by ships' gunfire during these forays.

Iceberg's L-Day had been successful beyond all expectation. For the entire day's operations, the Tenth Army suffered twenty-eight men killed, 104 wounded, and twenty-seven missing. Any sanguine hope

Corsair
The Vought F4U series of fighters, named the Corsair, was one of the 'greats' of air fighting in the Second World War. Fast, rugged and packing a great punch with its six machine guns and considerable bomb load, the Corsair was at first rejected by the US Navy as a carrier-borne fighter as a result of its high landing speed. After its success with the US Marines and carrier use in the Royal Navy, however, the Corsair was accepted by the US Navy. The accompanying illustration shows an F4U-1D Corsair. *Engine:* Pratt & Whitney R-2800, 2,000 hp. *Armament:* Six .5-inch machine guns plus two 1,000-pound bombs or eight 5-inch rockets. *Maximum speed:* 417 mph at 19,900 feet. *Rate of climb:* 2,890 feet per minute. *Ceiling:* 36,900 feet. *Range:* 1,015 miles normal. *Weights empty/loaded:* 8,982/14,000 pounds. *Span:* 41 feet. *Length:* 33 feet 4 inches

that the rest of the campaign would see as few American casualties was doomed within a few days into April.

After a relatively quiet night, punctuated only by slight sniper, machine gun, and mortar fire, the Tenth Army resumed the attack at 0730 on 2nd April. Perfect weather and light resistance faced the Americans this day and the next as Buckner's troops advanced swiftly across the island to take assigned objectives.

On the left flank of the Tenth Army line, 1/29 began clearing operations to Zampa Misaki, the peninsula northwest of Hagushi, for Turner wanted to establish a radar site on this point once it had been captured. He also wanted the beaches in this area uncovered in order that he might begin unloading operations here. By 1025, the Marines had seized the beaches and found them unsuitable for use by III Amphibious Corps.

The 4th Marines, on the 6th Division right, advanced through rugged terrain, meeting increasingly stiffer resistance as the day wore on. In the 1st Marine Division zone, the 7th and 5th Marines – from left to right

on line – moved out in order and pushed through the slight resistance offered by local defense units. During the day, IIIAC units killed over 900 Japanese and captured twenty-six.

Still, no contact had been made with enemy regular forces. An increasing number of dazed civilians began filtering through both Army and Marine lines. They were interrogated, screened, and sent back to stockades in the Tenth Army rear. Even though the Okinawans proved cooperative, little intelligence of immediate tactical value was gained. It was learned, however, that the Japanese had withdrawn to the south. In addition, intelligence personnel obtained some order of battle information and learned which areas the rest of the civilian populace had fled to.

In the XXIV Corps zone on the second day of the operation, troops of the 7th Division's 17th Infantry gained the highlands overlooking Nakagusuku Bay, and some regimental patrols even advanced to the shores of the east coast. To the right (south) of the division line, once the 32nd Infantry had reduced an enemy

Above: First casualties; the Marines overrun the West Beach wall
Left: Machine gun on the southern front

strongpoint south of Koza with tanks, it drew up abreast of the 17th Infantry. The 96th Division on the extreme right flank found slow going on L plus 1 also. The terrain over which it had to advance was rugged and marked with hills, abandoned caves and dugouts, mines, and tank traps. By the end of the day, Bradley's division had pushed out to the east and south, and succeeded in penetrating irregularly defended positions, some merely consisting of road mines and boobytrapped obstacles. By nightfall, the 96th Division's front lines extended from Futema on the west coast to approximately one mile north of Unjo in the east.

During the day, the 6th Engineer Battalion repaired the strips on Yontan and one taxiway was in good enough condition by 1500 to permit a spotter plane from Marine Observation 6 (VM 0–6) to land. By 4th April, all three Yontan runways were ready to take emergency landings.

At the close of 2nd April, all assault division command posts had been established ashore and the beachhead area and the bulk of the high ground behind the beaches firmly secured. Enemy observation of Tenth Army movement and dispositions thus became limited, and any Japanese land-based threat to unloading operations removed.

Even more of a problem than that posed by the inability of the ground forces to come to grips with the main enemy body was the dislocation of the logistics plan and subsequent strain on supporting units resulting from the swift and unopposed Tenth Army advances. The logistics annex of the operation plan had been based on the premise that the landings would be stubbornly resisted and unloading priorities were assigned accordingly. When the uncontested landing permitted the immediate debarkation of troops not scheduled to go ashore until 2nd or 3rd April, landing craft originally assigned to move cargo were diverted for the troop movement. As a result, the unloading of supplies on L-Day was delayed.

Shortly after the initial landings, Radio Tokyo had blithely predicted that the American beachhead on Okinawa would be wiped out. From 1st April on, however, the massive flow of troops and supplies ashore gave little credence to this optimistic enemy forecast. As assault units fanned out across the island – and in fact severed it on L plus 1 – shore party units took control of their assigned beach sectors.

While the Hagushi beaches varied widely in suitability, they were all generally adaptable to unloading operations. The only real obstacle to these operations was a coral reef extending the length of the beaches. Only during floodtime, a four-to-five-hour period, could landing craft such as the LCVPs and LCMs make direct runs to the shore. Low tide, however, exposed the coral outcroppings and forced Tenth Army logistics agencies to establish reef transfer points to maintain the flow of supplies and transfer of cargo. DUKWs and LVTs could negotiate the run from ship to shore at all times.

To get the cargo ships emptied sooner and to clear the beaches more quickly, on L plus 1 Turner authorized the use of floodlights for night-time unloading operations. Work was interrupted and the lights went out only when the early air raid warning net reported enemy aircraft headed for the transport area and the beaches. By 4th April, the effort to bridge the reef barrier off Hagushi beaches bore fruit. In place opposite Yontan airfield at Red Beach 1 were pontoon causeways that had been sidelifted to the target by LSTs. Earthfill ramps were constructed across the reef to Purple Beach 1 and Orange Beaches 1 and 2 near Kadena. In the mouth of the Bishi Gawa close to Yellow Beach 3, a small sand spit had been smoothed and enlarged. Engineers and Seabees then cut a loop access road through the beach cliff to the bar. Once these facilities were ready, cargo from landing craft as large as and including LCTs could be unloaded directly over the two causeways and the improved sandbar. Some eighty self-propelled barges, also side-lifted to Okinawa or carried on board cargo ships, were soon put to immediate use in a variety

of tasks. About twenty-five barges, equipped with cranes, were used to transfer cargo at the reef line; more were employed as lighters, others were transformed into petroleum barges, and still others used to evacuate casualties.

All Tenth Army shore party operations were placed in the hands of the Island Commander, Major-General Wallace, on 9th April, when his 1st Engineer Special Brigade assumed control of all beaches. One exception was the beach at Nago, which supported the activities of the far-ranging units of the 6th Marine Division as they advanced up the Ishikawa Isthmus and into northern Okinawa.

On 3rd April, both Tenth Army flanking units began flaring out to the north and south. In the XXIV Corps zone, Army forces had reached the east coast of Okinawa in force and Hodges' two combat divisions began regrouping and reorienting their attack to the south. The 7th Division had secured Awashi Peninsula and, pivoting in a clockwise movement coordinated with the 96th Division, gained another 3,000 yards before setting in night defenses. Near Kubasaki, the 32nd Infantry came up against its first real opposition on Okinawa, when, running into an enemy force of about 385 men, defeated them to take the objective. After the 96th Division completed its wheel to the right, it reorganized its front lines and was in position to jump off in the new axis of attack the next day.

To the north of the corps boundary, the 1st Marine Division had advanced 3,000-5,000 yards in its drive to the east coast, placing del Valle's troops eight to thirteen days ahead of the Iceberg schedule. By the end of the same day, Shepherd's 6th Division Marines had ground through heavily broken terrain, honeycombed with numerous caves, to gain 3,000-7,000 yards along its front line. At sundown, the division left flank was anchored on the base of Ishikawa Isthmus, thereby placing the Tenth

Rest and repair after the beach landing

Army twelve days ahead of its planned schedule in this area.

Because of the very favorable tactical situation that had developed in the III Amphibious Corps zone on 3rd April and as the 6th Marine Division approached the Nakadomari-Ishikawa line, Buckner sent a message to Geiger, 'All restrictions removed on your advance northwards.' This directive marked an important change in the conduct of the Iceberg operation, for the capture of Motobu Peninsula and northern Okinawa were originally scheduled to be part of Phase II of Iceberg. And now, Phase II was to begin before Phase I – operations involving the seizure of southern Okinawa – had barely begun.

Tank-mounted 6th Division infantry columns immediately dashed up both coastal coasts and foot troops slogged straight up the central portion of the isthmus against slight opposition, negligible man-made and natural obstacles, and very rugged mountainous terrain. In ten days, the 6th Division gained more than twenty-five miles to the mouth of the Motobu Peninsula. Once the 22nd Marines had captured Hedo Misaki, the northernmost point of Okinawa on 13th April, all Marine efforts could be concentrated on the main objective, Yae Take on Motobu Peninsula, the center of Japanese resistance in the north. Although supply lines had been strained to their utmost, the opening of unloading beaches at Nago on the 9th reduced the road traffic coming from Hagushi and permitted LSTs and other cargo-carrying vessels and craft to support the Marines more directly and fully.

Motobu Peninsula and the enemy order of battle here were virtually unknown factors as the 6th Division approached Colonel Udo's mountain bastion on Yae Take. Heavy cloud cover had obscured the interior of the north when the first photo-reconnaissance missions were flown, and in any case, dense vegetation covering the trails and terrain contours would have made it impossible to interpret the photographs thus obtained if they had been any good in the first place. Not until a Japanese map of the area had been captured did the Japanese situation become apparent.

As the Marines entered the Peninsula, it widened out and the inland terrain rose sharply in a series of sharp slopes. Towering over all of this was Yae Take, whose heights reached 1,500 feet in places. All in all, the ground heavily favored the defenders, who had organized it to its best advantage. Udo was superbly well prepared to undertake the mission he had been assigned by Thirty-second Army. He thoroughly knew the area he was to defend, had excellent outposts guarding his main position, and was in good communication with his outlying troops. For their part, the Japanese soldiers on Motobu also were quite familiar with the terrain they were defending and could move about quite freely on the horses they had been provided with or had liberated from the Okinawans.

The enemy defense about Yae Take consisted of small, concealed groups which acted as a screen to the main battle position. Every possible stratagem was employed to delay and disorganize the Marine attack, and to lead the Marines away from the center of Udo's defense. Japanese soldiers lay in wait in hidden positions with their weapons zeroed in on open portions of the trail. They held their fire until a sizable American force passed by, and then opened up when a choice target came into their sights. As a result, many Marine officers fell prey to the enemy snipers.

Marine confirmation of the location of the main enemy force, whose whereabouts and strength to this point had been somewhat conjectural, was acquired on the night of 12th-13th April. At this time, Shepherd's troops encountered some English-speaking Okinawans who had formerly lived in Hawaii. These natives identified Udo's force and gave added validity to the information already gained from captured documents. Put together, this intelligence showed that enemy troop strength was close to 1,500 men. Included in this so-called Udo Force, were infantry, machine gun units, light and medium artillery, Okinawan conscripts, and naval personnel from the Unten-Ko bases. In addition to 75mm and 150mm artillery pieces, Udo had two 6-inch naval guns capable of

Above: Marine Corsairs on rocket-strike mission. *Below:* Corsair fires its sheaf of missiles at hill targets

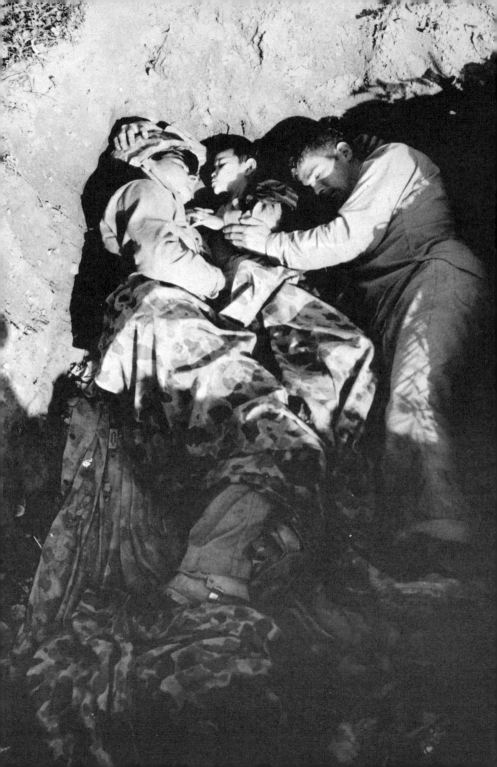

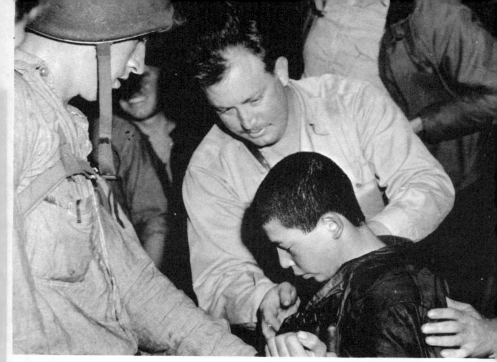

Left: Battle weary Marines share foxhole with war orphan. *Above:* Japanese airman picked up by US destroyers; eight others swam away, refusing rescue
Below: Candy and sympathy for aged woman of Okinawa

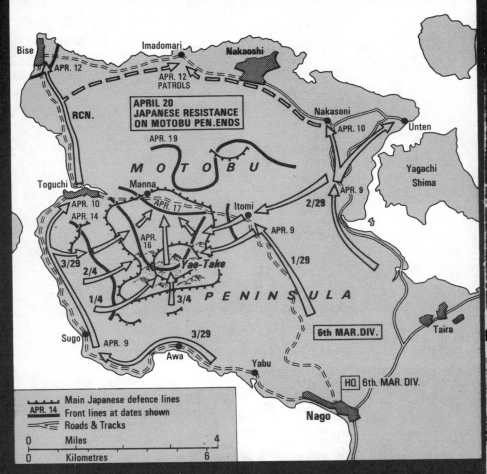

The Motobu Peninsula campaign

bearing on the coastal road for a distance of ten miles south of Motobu, on Ie Shima, and all of Nago and its beaches.

The Marine attack against Yae Take began on 14th April, when two battalions of Shapley's 4th Marines, with 3/29 attached, attacked eastward from Toguchi and seized a 700-foot-high ridge about 1,200 yards inland and dominating the west coast and its coastal road. By evening the Marines had a firm grip on their objective. Utilizing their excellent observation of all American movement and their equally good fields of fire, the Japanese poured down machine gun, small arms, and mortar fire on the advancing Marines, but did not slow them up appreciably. In a squeeze play, the remaining two battalions of the 29th Marines made an approach march from Itomi to occupy the high hills overlooking the Itomi-Manna road. It became a small-unit commander's war at this point, a war of fire and maneuver, as the rugged terrain precluded rigid control by senior commanders. Each battalion and company commander had to devise his own method of approach up the ravines, valleys, and steep hills to the objective. In face of enemy objection to their approach to Yae Take, the two battalions of the 29th Marines were diverted to the southwest, and spent the next three days probing Japanese positions, while relieving the main attack of some of the enemy pressure, to a degree.

After day-long maneuvering and hand-to-hand fighting, at the end of 15th April, the reinforced 4th Marines force was in position for a final assault. Yae Take, at this point, was all but encircled from the west, south, and east. Although Marine casualties had been heavy, Japanese losses were the greater, for over 1,120 enemy dead had been counted and numerous other Japanese soldiers had been sealed in caves. Nonetheless, sensing that the end was not far off, early the next day, supported by air, artillery, and naval gunfire, 1/4 attacked up the steep southwestern slopes of Yae Take. Against a constant drumfire from rifles, machine guns, and hand grenades, the Marines gained the height of the crest.

The battle for this piece of real estate raged fiercely back and forth with neither side gaining an advantage until late afternoon, when the Marines won the day. At 1830, the Japanese counterattacked, but were repulsed with heavy losses, for 1/4 had been able to reinforce and resupply its troops on the height. Fortunately for the Americans, Udo's force was spent, and for the next two days, the remnants of his organization attempted to infiltrate Marine lines to head north, where the enemy commander planned to resort to guerrilla tactics.

While the main Japanese positions on Motobu had been captured, the northern and greater portion of Yae Take still remained in enemy hands. This situation was changed on the 17th, when 1/29 captured this territory. Meanwhile, the 4th Marines swept to the north over Yae Take and killed about 700 more Japanese in the process. On this day, Udo's abandoned command post and a large stock of Japanese stores were found, indicating that the enemy had indeed been chased from his once-impregnable position. Following up their success on Yae Take, the Marines began the the final drive to the northern coast of the peninsula on 19th April. With the 4th and 29th Marines abreast, and supported by Marine Corsairs armed with napalm, rockets, and bombs, the attack pushed forward against only slight resistance. These two regiments gained the coast the next day, when Shepherd reported the end of organised resistance on Motobu Peninsula. In fourteen days, the 6th Division had pushed to the northernmost point of Okinawa from its original landing beaches, a distance of some fifty-five miles. During seven days of this two-week period, the division had been involved in a successful mountain campaign conducted in some of the ruggedest terrain found on Okinawa. In the course of the fight to clear Motobu Peninsula, the 6th Marine Division lost 207 men killed, 757 wounded, and six missing in action. The Marines counted over 2,000 Japanese dead – soldiers whose lives were forfeited while they defended their positions with a tenacity that had come to be characteristic of the Imperial Japanese forces.

The battle continues

While the 6th Marine Division fought its way to the north, the 1st Division swept across the center of the island to the east coast, down the Katchin Peninsula, and even took the little island of Yabuchi Shima at the tip of the peninsula by 6th April. Once having seized all of this terrain against only slight resistance, del Valle's Marines began operations in the rear to clean up bypassed enemy pockets. XXXIV Corps troops at the same time aggressively exploited the same lack of enemy resistance, and by the night of L plus 4 had seized the L plus 10 Line, which originally had been designated as the southernmost limit of the Tenth Army beachhead.

The question uppermost in everyone's mind was: 'Where are the Japanese?' As in the north, cloud over the Shuri area and its environs served the enemy well, for it had masked from American photo-reconnaissance flights the true extent of Ushijima's defenses and the concentration of his strength here. According to the Thirty-second Army plan, Ushijima's troops had only to stand fast and wait for the Americans to come to them, and they were not to be disappointed. By the morning of 6th April, Hodge had a pretty good idea that Japanese 'lines were drawn for a full-scale battle.'

What the 7th and 96th Infantry Divisions were encountering was a strong enemy position that extended the width of the island roughly following an imaginary line running through Machinato, Kakazu, Kaniku, Minami-Uebaru, and Tsuwa. With flanks anchored on the East China Sea and the Pacific Ocean, this Japanese barrier was the outermost of a series of defense lines guarding Shuri, headquarters of Ushijima's army. Veteran troops of the 62nd Division were strongly entrenched in this outpost sector, comprised of well-prepared positions on high ground that was liberally studded with machine guns and mortars, and surrounded by barbed wire, antitank ditches, and minefields. In short time, XXIV Corps troops painfully learned that the enemy was prepared to fight a 'prolonged holding action' here.

As the battle for southern Okinawa gradually took form, it became neces-sary for the Tenth Army to ensure the security of its flanks by neutralizing the off-shore islands, notably the Eastern Islands guarding Chimu Wan on the east coast, and Ie Shima, almost directly opposite Motobu Peninsula on the west coast. Since the rapid sweep across Okinawa had cleared the shoreline of Chimu Wan and a large section of the upper portion of Naka-gusuku Wan, Turner was anxious to utilize these east coast areas for unloading operations as soon as possible. Although minesweepers had cleared the channels in these two bays, enemy strength on the six small islands guarding the mouths of the bays had to be determined before unloading operations could safely begin. To secure this information, the FMFPac Amphibious Reconnaissance Battalion was attached to the Eastern Islands Attack and Fire Support Group and given a mission of scouting the islands.

Beginning 0200, 6th April, the Marine scouts landed on Tsugen Shima, suspected of being the most heavily defended island of the group. Japanese reaction to this intrusion was almost immediate, and the Marines withdrew to the beaches under a hail of enemy mortar shells and machine gun fire. Because their mission had been to uncover, not engage, the Japanese troops here, the Americans reboarded the high-speed APDs and left the area to reconnoiter the other islands in the group. For the next two days and nights, the Marines scouted the remaining five islands with largely negative results. All they found were frightened civilians, and unmanned defensive positions.

The assignment for the capture of Tsugen Shima was then given to 3/105 of the 27th Infantry Division. Although the island had been pounded incessantly by air and naval gunfire since L-Day and before, it was made the target of an especially heavy preparation prior to the Army landing at 0840 on 10th April. The taking of Tsugen Shima was not an easy task, as the soldiers soon discovered, and the battle for this small island lasted all day and through the night, during

A scouting patrol advances up the mountain on Aka Shima

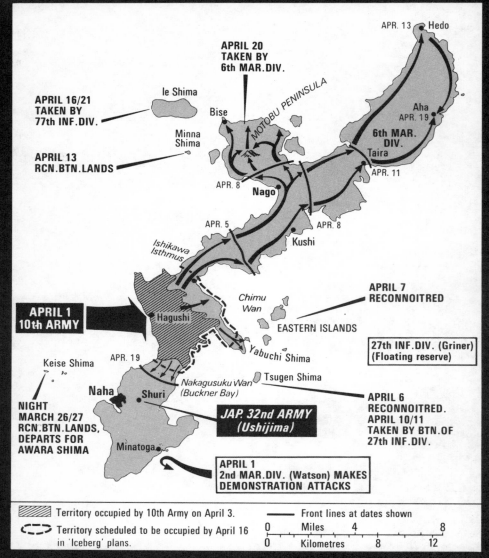

APRIL 13 • Hedo

APRIL 20
TAKEN BY
6th MAR.DIV.

APRIL 16/21
TAKEN BY
77th INF.DIV.

le Shima

Minna
Shima

APRIL 13
RCN.BTN.LANDS

Bise

MOTOBU PENINSULA

Aha
APR. 19

6th MAR.
DIV.

Taira

APR. 11

APR. 8

Nago

APR. 5

APR. 8

Kushi

Ishikawa
Isthmus

APRIL 7
RECONNOITRED

Chimu
Wan

EASTERN ISLANDS

27th INF.DIV. (Griner)
(Floating reserve)

APRIL 1
10th ARMY

Hagushi

Yabuchi Shima

Keise Shima

APR. 19

Tsugen Shima

Nakagusuku Wan
(Buckner Bay)

APRIL 6
RECONNOITRED.
APRIL 10/11
TAKEN BY BTN.OF
27th INF.DIV.

NIGHT
MARCH 26/27
RCN.BTN.LANDS,
DEPARTS FOR
AWARA SHIMA

Naha

Shuri

JAP. 32nd ARMY
(Ushijima)

Minatoga

APRIL 1
2nd MAR.DIV. (Watson) MAKES
DEMONSTRATION ATTACKS

▨▨▨ Territory occupied by 10th Army on April 3.

⊂⊃ Territory scheduled to be occupied by April 16
in 'Iceberg' plans.

—— Front lines at dates shown

0   Miles   4   8

0   Kilometres   8   12

Campaign developments up to 21st April

which time 3/105 suffered heavy casualties.

Organized resistance ended at 1530 on the 11th, when the survivors of the battalion were pulled off the island to rejoin their parent unit at Kerama Retto. In a day and a half of fighting, eleven Americans died, eighty were wounded, and three listed as missing. The enemy suffered even heavier casualties, for an estimated 234 were killed; no prisoners were taken.

The seizure of Tsugen opened the approaches to Nakagusuku Wan, and ensured that XXIV Corps units would receive supplies from east as well as west coast beaches. This action reduced the load on the Hagushi beaches, expedited base development on Okinawa, and hastened the construction of additional unloading facilities on the Pacific Ocean side of the island.

The capture of Ie Shima was a more complex operation with larger forces, took longer to accomplish, and was a somewhat costlier effort than the Tsugen Shima assault. Nonetheless, the Americans had to take Ie Shima because its size and physical characteristics permitted extensive airfield development, a factor which escaped the attention of neither Japanese nor American planners. As a matter of concern to Iceberg, the enemy had already laid out three runways – each a mile in length – on the central plateau of the island, and the plan for Okinawa called for the expansion of these existing strips as well as the addition of others which would eventually accommodate an entire wing of very long-range fighter aircraft.

Because Motobu Peninsula and northern Okinawa had been taken after an overland attack rather than by amphibious assault, Iceberg commanders were able to make use of available transports and fire support ships to mount the assault on Ie Shima. Losing no time, Turner issued the attack order directing the seizure of the island and designated the Northern Attack Force commander, Rear-Admiral Reifsnider, as Commander, Ie Shima Attack Group.

Assigned as the landing force for this phase of Iceberg was the 77th Infantry Division. Following its successful Kerama Retto operation, this unit spent approximately two weeks on board ships in a convoy which steamed in circles about 300 miles southeast of Okinawa. Despite its distance from the scene of the major fighting, the division was not out of action long. On 2nd April in a surprise attack, Japanese suicide planes dove out of a large cloud band which had hidden their approach, and crashed four ships in the convoy before ships' anti-aircraft fire could open up. Three of these vessels were command ships, on one of which was the 305th Infantry's regimental staff, which was killed or wounded to a man. Nevertheless, this regiment and its parent division was committed to the Ie Shima operation scheduled for 16th April.

As in the Kerama Retto and Eastern Islands attacks, the Marine Reconnaisance Battalion again was scheduled to conduct preliminary operations. Its mission this time was to seize and occupy Minna Shima, a small, crescent-shaped island about 6,000 yards southeast of the primary objective. The Marines landed on 13th April and swept the island in two hours' time, finding only thirty civilians. Shortly thereafter, 77th Division artillery was landed, emplaced, and ready to provide supporting fire for the rest of the division when it landed on Ie Shima.

The preliminary bombardment of the target began at dawn on 16th April and was stepped up at 0725, when missions in direct support of the landing were fired. Both naval gunfire and air support were provided for the assaulting division, and although there was little initial opposition to the landing, it was not too long afterwards before enemy resistance stiffened. By mid-afternoon, delaying groups, which had been concealed in caves and fortified tombs, began contesting every yard of the soldiers' advance. For six days the 77th Division struggled, in many cases fighting hand-to-hand with defenders unwilling to yield. As the battle unfolded, it was discovered that Japanese defenses were centered about Iegusugu Yama, and the small village of Ie which lay at the foot of the southern slope of this mountain.

The Ie Shima garrison had per-

Above: Okinawan civilians undergo registration. *Left:* Columnist Ernie Pyle rests with a Marine patrol

formed a masterful camouflage job, for nearly 7,000 troops were concealed on the island. Iegusugu Yama contained a maze of hidden firing positions and Ie itself had been converted into a veritable fortress. The route of advance to the core of enemy defenses was across open land, uphill all the way, and flanked by Japanese positions in the village, and overall dominated by concrete emplacements located in a reinforced concrete building on a steep rise which faced the attacking troops. The American infantry soon named this structure 'Government House,' and the terrain on which it stood, 'Bloody Ridge.'

On 20th April, after a grim bayonet and grenade attack, the top of Bloody Ridge was finally gained and Government House taken. The island was declared secure on 21st April after the 77th Division had won a victory for which a heavy price was exacted – 239 men killed, 879 wounded, and

nineteen missing. Japanese losses were 4,706 killed and 149 captured.

During the next four days, scattered Japanese and Okinawan soldiers were hunted down, and on the 25th, LSTs began shuttling division units to Okinawa, where their extra strength was needed in helping the XXIV Corps press the attack on Shuri defenses. Remaining in garrison on Ie Shima were the regimental headquarters and the 1st Battalion of the 30th Infantry. This force was considered adequate to handle the rest of the cleanup operations on the island.

One of the many ironies of the Okinawa campaign is the fact that it was on miniscule Ie Shima that famed war correspondent Ernie Pyle – the GI's spokesman – was killed. This accomplished newspaperman had experienced the worst of the Italian campaign with Army troops and had journeyed across the Pacific to see what the island war was like. While on his way to the front in a jeep on 18th April with a regimental commander, a Japanese machine gun nest in the terraced slopes on the outskirts of Ie opened up, sending both men into a nearby ditch. When Pyle raised his head above the edge of the ditch a few minutes later, another burst 'caught him full in the temple just below the rim of his helmet, killing him instantly.' He was buried later in the 77th Division's cemetery on Ie under a crude marker which the division later replaced with a monument, on which is inscribed: 'At this spot the 77th Infantry Division lost a buddy, Ernie Pyle, 18th April 1945.'

As a sidelight to the air battle over and the land fighting on Okinawa, the Japanese mounted their only real surface threat to the success of the American invasion. Intending to attack Allied shipping at Okinawa, the battleship *Yamato* and a covering group steamed out of Honshu's Tokuyama Naval Base at 1500 on 6th April. The 69,110-ton vessel was a real giant of the seas, for its primary armament consisted of nine 18-inch rifles which could out-gun any ship in the Allied naval force. This Japanese behemoth could cruise for a distance of 7,200 sea miles at a steady sixteen knots before need of refueling. It had an

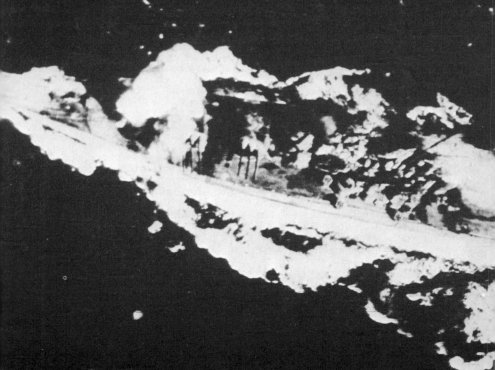

The battleship *Yamato*. *Above:* in 1941.
Below: damaged she flees from units
of the US Third Fleet

overall length of 863 feet and a beam
of 128 feet, and carried a crew of
2,500 men.

The sortie of the *Yamato* and its
covering force of one light cruiser and
eight destroyers was planned to aid
the *Kamikaze* attacks on American
shipping in the Hagushi anchorage.
Provided with only enough fuel for a
one-way voyage, the giant battleship's mission was to shell the landing area and anchorage at Okinawa in
order to draw off American air cover
and give the suicide planes a clear
shot at the amphibious force. There
was little doubt that this was a
suicide mission and Admiral Soemu
Toyoda, commander of the Japanese
Combined Fleet, believed the *Yamato*
group to have less than an even chance
of ever reaching its target. Task
Force 58 elements reduced these odds
even more.

Less than two hours after the
Yamato group had made open sea,
the submarines *Hackleback* and
Threadfin, lying off the east coast of
Kyushu, discovered these lucrative
targets and alerted the Fifth Fleet at
about 1710. The subs lost their contact later that night, but a search
plane from the carrier *Essex* picked up
the enemy ships again at 0822 on the
7th. At 1030, Kerama-based PBYs
began tracking the *Yamato* group
and at the same time the last of
three strike groups – a total of 380
planes – was launched by TF 58. The
American attack began at 1210 with
the bombing of a destroyer lagging at
the rear of the Japanese formation.
A half hour later the full fury of the
first two groups hit the main enemy
force. *Yamato* took two bombs and a
torpedo, another destroyer was sunk,
and the cruiser was stopped dead in
the water. At 1333 the third group
struck and finished the job in less
than an hour. Three additional bombs
and nine torpedos hit the *Yamato*
which then capsized, blew up, and
sank a full day's steaming from Okinawa. The cruiser and one other
destroyer were likewise sunk. Later
that night, a fourth destroyer, heavily
damaged, was scuttled as the remaining ships withdrew to Japan –
mission not accomplished.

The war
in the air

While this venture in support of *Kamikaze* operations ended in dismal failure, the Japanese high command was convinced of the efficacy of suicide missions. Orders were issued to the Fifth Air Fleet 'to continue general attacks at all costs.' As the battle was joined on Okinawa by the Tenth and Thirty-second Armies, the American fleet in surrounding waters found itself engaged in a desperate struggle of its own. The Japanese air attacks on the Kerama Retto invasion group prior to L-Day merely heralded even greater enemy attempts to destroy the surface forces supporting and guarding the troops on Okinawa. Many of these enemy aircraft were on either conventional bombing or reconnaissance missions; others in the aerial attacks were part of the Japanese Special Attack Force, the *Kamikazes*.

Americans first experienced the *Kamikaze* phenomenon in the Philippines, where MacArthur's air elements reigned supreme in the skies overhead. Japanese naval commanders soon saw that they could not expect to gain any advantage in the air while their squadrons continuedly employed orthodox tactics against the Allies. The *Kamikaze* effort resulted from these considerations, and quite simply represented a desperate attempt by suicide-bent Japanese naval aviators to deprive American invasion shipping of its air cover by crashing the flattops of the accompanying carrier forces. Although Japanese commanders believed that suicide missions were a 'temporary expedient' only, used 'because we were incapable of combating' the Americans 'by other means . . .' initial successes enabled the enemy to rationalize the use of *Kamikazes* more fully both in the Philippines and elsewhere.

At the outset, a combined force of about 1,815 planes was assigned to carry out well-planned and organized suicide raids at Okinawa – a decided contrast to the sporadic, albeit somewhat successful, *Kamikaze* attacks at Leyte. Scattered suicide and conventional flights from Japan and Formosa carried the attack to the Western Islands Attack Group of the Iceberg force first. Later these planes began swarming all over the transports and radar picket line off Okinawa.

During the first few days of April, the toll of damaged and sunk ships grew at an alarming rate while naval casualties mounted in proportion. By 6th April, Admiral Toyoda was prepared to launch from Kyushu the first of ten carefully planned *Kamikaze* flights to be flown over a period of weeks ending 22nd June. The attacks 'were given the cover name *Kikusui . . .*' which 'literally means "chrysanthemum water" and the characters making up the word were used in the crest of a Fifteenth Century Japanese hero who took the side of the Emperor in a prolonged civil war against heavy odds.' Before these attacks ended, a total of 1,465 flights emanated from Kyushu to sink twenty-six American ships and damage 164 others. Not included in these loss figures are the victims of small-scale *Kamikaze* efforts by another 250 planes which rose from fields on Formosa and an additional 185 sorties flown from Kyushu independent of the mass attacks.

The Japanese decision to turn to large-scale air operations was arrived at after Admiral Toyoda studied the situations facing both his forces and those of the Thirty-second Army, and he found that 'it would be futile to turn the tide of battle with present tactics.' He therefore ordered the first and largest coordinated suicide attack, *Kikusui* Operation No 1, unleashed against Iceberg forces on 6th April. Spearheading the *Kamikazes* were fourteen planes sent to bomb and strafe Okinawa airfields before dawn to destroy Allied aircraft suspected of being there. Aside from their nuisance value, the raids did little damage to the runways, and none to Tactical Air Force planes, for none had flown ashore yet. Following this first group of hecklers were more than one hundred fighters and bombers sent to engage TF 58 off Amami-O-Shima in order to draw American carrier-based planes away from the suiciders heading for Okinawa.

Vessels stricken by *Kamikaze* planes. *Above:* USS *Tennessee*. *Below:* USS LCT-447

For a thirty-six hour period during 6th to 7th April, the Japanese flew 355 suicide sorties, accompanied by a nearly equal number of conventional cover, reconnaissance, and bombing planes. As these aircraft bore in to crash, torpedo, and bomb the ships at anchor in the Hagushi transport area, crewmen in exposed positions and troops on the beaches were subjected to a deadly rain of antiaircraft artillery shell fragments. Friendly fighters from the carriers also came under the fire of the hundreds of guns on the ships and emplaced ashore. Three American pilots were shot down when they followed Japanese planes too closely into the murderous barrage.

The main attack, beginning about 1500 on 6th April, spread out all over the combat zone with the outer ring of radar pickets and patrol craft – lacking a protective smoke-screen cover – catching the full brunt of the enemy planes. Ships of all types, however, were fair game for the *Kamikazes*. Amongst the vessels hit in the Kerama anchorage were two cargo ships loaded on the west coast of the United States with all the 81mm mortar ammunition then available.

Fortunately, this shortage was made up before the end of the Okinawa campaign by airlifted shipments.

In this first mass suicide attack, Turner's pilots claimed to have shot down at least 135 enemy planes, while the pilots from the Fast Carrier Task Force reported splashing 245 more, bringing the total American claims of enemy losses to nearly 400 pilots and planes. Contemporary Japanese sources list the losses in *Kikusui* number 1 at 335.

Since TAF pilots had not yet begun operations from Okinawa when this attack began, carrier-based Navy and Marine squadrons conducted air defense of the island until Mulcahy's force arrived. The TAF commander and his headquarters went ashore on 2nd April and selected a command post site midway between Yontan and Kadena airfields. Wallace's Air Defense Command was established nearby. Although hurried grading permitted emergency use of Yontan by 7th April, Kadena had been more extensively damaged and repair to its strips was not completed until the 9th, and then only for use in dry weather.

Above left : Abandoned Japanese suicide boat. *Above:* Marine Avengers
Below : Rocket powered *'Baka* bomb' suicide plane left at Kadena field

Wallace believed that the major tactical task of his ADC was to meet the *Kamikaze* threat. From 7th April, when Marine Fighter Squadron 311 (VMF-311) pilots flying in to Yontan from their escort carrier lift scored the first TAF kill of a suicider, ADC efforts were directed toward confronting and stopping the destructive enemy air attacks. The fighter squadrons of Marine Aircraft Groups 31 and 33 (MAG-31 and 33) mounted combat air patrols from Yontan and Kadena fields from the first days they arrived at these bases.

Almost as soon as Colonel John C Munn's MAG-31 touched down at Yontan and was refueled, a twelve plane combat air patrol was organized and launched to remain airborne until dusk. Basically, the aircraft were deployed in a circle in depth over the invasion force shipping and the picket craft. Generally, TAF planes were airborne from dawn to dusk on CAP flights, and flew special early morning and twilight CAPs as well. When the radar-equipped night fighters of Marine Night Fighter Squadrons 542 and 543 arrived at Okinawa, TAF was directed to establish and maintain a four plane CAP constantly during the hours of darkness. The mission of the TAF pilots was two-fold – they were to defend Tenth Army ground units against Japanese incursions from the air and to protect Fifth Fleet shipping as well as the radar pickets.

For both Marine ground and air elements in the Tenth Army, it was somewhat of an incongruity that TAF Marine squadrons, based on Okinawa fields, should be flying the combat air patrols, while close air support of the ground troops – a specialty of Marine pilots – was provided by Navy flyers based on the carriers. To at least one TAF air group commander, 'it seemed strange for planes off the carriers to come in for close-support missions, passing Marine pilots flying out for CAP duty . . .' At any rate, the Marine Landing Force Air Control Support Units, which landed shortly after TAF went ashore on Okinawa, coordinated and monitored all Tenth Army requests for close air support missions. Front-line control of the ground missions

flown both by land- and carrier-based aircraft was provided by the Air Liaison Parties from Joint Assault Signal Companies attached to each infantry division.

As TAF fighter pilots added to their expanding bag of downed enemy planes, other types of air missions in support of the Tenth Army were performed by Mulcahy's command. Upon its arrival in the battle zone, the Army Air Forces' 28th Photo Reconnaissance Squadron rephotographed the entire Okinawa Gunto area to obtain more accurate and complete coverage than had been available for the maps used on L-Day. As soon as Marine Torpedo Bomber Squadron 232 arrived on 22nd April, it was given tasks other than its original mission of antisubmarine warfare. During the remainder of the month, the squadron flew numerous artillery observation missions daily, bombed and strafed enemy lines and installations in southern Okinawa, and conducted heckling raids in these same areas almost nightly.

During 12th-13th April, the second mass *Kamikaze* attack took place. Although as frenzied and almost as destructive as the first *Kikusui*, it was mounted by only 392 planes, on both conventional and suicide missions, as opposed to the 699 planes in the first attack. As they did during the first attack, TF 58 pilots downed

The MXY-8 Missile
Named Okha (Cherry Blossom) by the Japanese and Baka (Fool) by the Americans, the MXY-8 Model 11 was designed as a cheaply-produced expendable suicide missile for use against the numerically superior and technically more advanced Allied forces advancing on Japan toward the end of the war.
Specification: *Engine:* Type 4 Mark 1 Model 20 solid fuel rockets (three in number), 1,764 lbs of thrust in total. *Maximum speed:* 570 mph. *Range:* 50 miles when launched at 27,000 feet. *Armament:* A high explosive warhead of 2,645 pounds weight. *Span:* 16 feet 5 inches. *Length:* 19 feet 8½ inches

most of the enemy, while Okinawa-based TAF flyers accounted for sixteen planes in this raid. TAF reports evaluating this second suicide raid noted that the evasive tactics employed by the enemy did 'not tend to indicate that the flyers were top-flight fighter pilots,' and that 'a definite lack of aggressiveness' seemed to confirm the belief that 'the pilots were green.'

A third mass raid of 498 aircraft (196 of which were suiciders) hit Okinawa 15th-16th April. As the wild air battle carried over into the second day, TAF planes began to score heavily. In this attack, a Marine pilot first sighted the so-called 'Baka' bomb in its maiden appearance over Okinawa. This small, rocket-powered wooden craft, carried a one-man crew and over a ton and half of explosive. Carried by a twin-engine bomber to a point near the target, the Baka was released when its pilot had verified the weapon's target and

position, oriented his own position, and started the rocket motors. Although the destructive powers of the Baka were quite real, its employment was erratic and it appeared too late in the war to influence its course.

TAF operations for the rest of April tended to fall into a routine of combat air patrols and support missions. The fourth mass *Kamikaze* raid of the month took place on 27th-28th April, when 115 Japanese suicide pilots attacked friendly shipping and the steadfast radar pickets. Late in the afternoon of the second day, another *Kamikaze* formation was intercepted by TAF pilots as it approached Okinawa. As in the case of the other attacks, all the enemy planes were either shot down or driven off, with most of the latter not making their home fields. By the end of April, TAF pilots had flown 3,521 CAP sorties and had shot down or assisted in the downing of 143 enemy aircraft.

The Shuri barrier

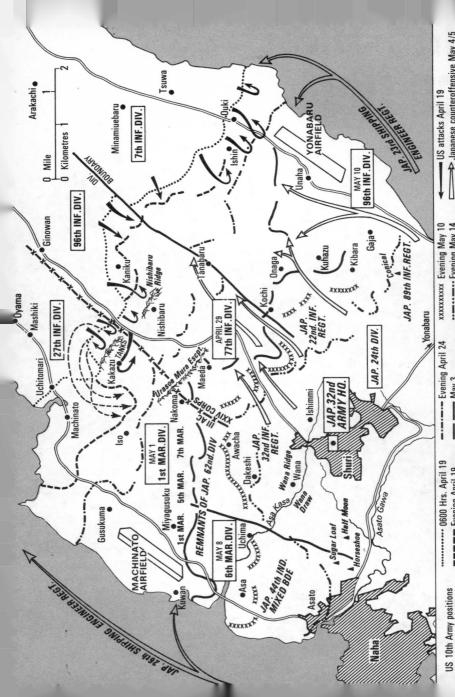

Arakachi●

0 Mile · 1
0 Kilometres · 1 · 2

Tsuwa●

Minamiuebaru●

7th INF. DIV.

Duki●

Ishin●

YONABARU AIRFIELD

MAY 10 96th INF. DIV.

JAP. 23rd SHIPPING ENGINEER REGT.

Ginowan●

96th INF. DIV.

DIV BOUNDARY

Kaniku●

Nishibaru Ridge

Tanabaru●

Unaha●

Oyama●

Mashiki●

27th INF. DIV.

Nishibaru●

Kochi●

Onaga▲

Kunazu●

Kibara●

Gaja●

conical▲

Uchitomari●

Kakazu TANKS

Maeda●

Urasoe Mura Esepl.

XXXX · XXXX

APRIL 29 77th INF. DIV.

JAP. 22nd INF. REGT.

JAP. 89th INF. REGT.

Machinato●

Iso●

Nakoma

III AC XXX

XXIV CORPS

Awacha

Dakeshi●

JAP. 32nd INF. REGT.

Ishimmi●

JAP. 32nd ARMY HQ.

Shuri

JAP. 24th DIV.

Yonabaru●

Gusukuma●

MAY 1 1st MAR. DIV.

7th MAR.

5th MAR.

Wana Ridge

Wana

Miyagusuku●

1st MAR.

Asa Kasa

Wana Draw

REMNANTS OF JAP. 62nd DIV.

Uchima●

Asato Gawa

Kuwan●

MACHINATO AIRFIELD

MAY 8 6th MAR. DIV.

●Asa

Sugar Loaf▲

▲Half Moon

▲Horseshoe

JAP. 44th IND. MIXED BDE

Asato●

JAP. 26th SHIPPING ENGINEER REGT.

Naha

US 10th Army positions

·········· 0600 Hrs. April 19
― ― ― Evening April 19

― · ― Evening April 24
――― May 3

xxxxxxxx Evening May 10
·····x···· Evening May 14

――→ US attacks April 19
⇒ Japanese counteroffensive May 4/5

In the days immediately following the facing movement of the XXIV Corps and the beginning of its drive to the south, increasingly stiff and bitter resistance gave proof that the prepared enemy defenses were being uncovered. The nature of the contacts with the Japanese also gave proof of the end of the relatively easy and fast-moving Army advance. Limited Army gains were registered on 7th April, as one 96th Division battalion approached to within 500 yards of Kakazu after a fierce fight supported by three air strikes, four artillery battalions, and the 14-inch rifles of the *New York*. During the night of 7th-8th April, the Japanese made some minor infiltration attempts all along the XXIV Corps line, but they were handily repulsed with little effort by the Americans.

Heavy winds and torrential rains marked 8th April and again on the following day, when the 96th Division pushed hard against Kakazu Ridge, which the Americans had determined was a key feature of the Shuri defense system. Frequent enemy counterattacks and withering fire forced the soldiers to relinquish what slight gains they had made and, at the end of each day, to withdraw to original jump-off positions. On L plus 9, all three infantry regiments of the 96th Division attacked following a massive thirty-minute artillery and naval gunfire preparation on the objective. The net result at the end of this day was a gain of only 300 yards. A Japanese counterattack at midnight of 12th April was thrown back, and two lesser ones again mounted against XXIV Corps on the night of 13th-14th April were easily blunted by means of heavy mortar and small arms fire. For their efforts in these two days, the Japanese suffered 1,584 troops killed and four captured.

Ushijima had planned to mount these counterattacks in greater force and timed to coincide with a *Kamikaze* attack on 6th April, but cancellation of the suicide raid forced the enemy ground effort to be cancelled similarly. A partial explanation for the failure of the subsequent attacks is found in the strength of American reaction to them. In addition, Colonel Yahara, Thirty-second Army Operations Officer, had recommended that only a few shock troops be committed rather than a major force. His opposition to these attacks stemmed from his belief that they were not in keeping with the defensive mission of the Thirty-second Army and that they would result in a sheer waste of Japanese manpower. He was proved right, for the attacks were very costly to the enemy, who concluded that the night assaults 'resulted in complete failure.'

While the enemy had accomplished absolutely nothing in his fruitless counterattacks, XXIV Corps units had been similarly stymied in their effort to advance against Shuri, which had begun to take on the aura of an unconquerable bastion. Although the question regarding the location of Japanese forces was only beginning to be resolved, Tenth Army intelligence sections were quite certain that the bulk of the Thirty-second Army had not yet been met.

The nature of the Shuri defense demanded from the first the fullest possible employment of every weapon available to the infantry. Artillery especially was needed to reduce prepared Japanese positions and to denude them of their skillfully designed camouflage, to seal off the firing ports, and to collapse the labyrinth of interconnecting tunnels that housed and protected the defending troops. To beef up his XXIV Corps Artillery and organic divisional artillery, Hodges requested and was given additional firing batteries, all of them coming from the Marine III Amphibious Corps Artillery and the 1st Marine Division during the period 9th-12th April. Moving south at the same time was the 27th Infantry Division (less the 105th Regimental Combat Team), which entered the XXIV Corps lines on 15th April.

It was at the end of the second week on Okinawa, on Friday 13th April (12th April in the States), Iceberg forces learned of the death of President Franklin D Roosevelt. Memorial services were held on board American vessels and behind Tenth Army lines. Those who could attend these services did so if the fighting permitted.

Network of tracer anti-aircraft fire in a Japanese raid on Yontan airfield

Because Hodges was well aware that a maximum effort would be needed if Thirty-second Army lines were to be broken, he scheduled a corps attack, three divisions abreast, for 19th April. Beginning on the 15th, four days were spent in preparation for the push. While all guns and howitzers smashed enemy positions to the front and troop concentration areas in the rear, an American supply build-up was underway. In this pre-attack period, planes from TAF, and Task Forces 51, 52, and 58 flew a total of 905 sorties in direct support missions for XXIV Corps. The pilots dropped 482 tons of bombs, and expended 3,400 rockets and over 700,000 rounds of .50 caliber and 20mm ammunition on Japanese installations. Added to this firepower was that coming from the strong force of TF 51 battleships, cruisers, and destroyers remaining on call offshore both day and night.

Prior to the attack, front line units attempted to improve their positions with small local attacks, while patrols were sent forward to pinpoint enemy positions and weapons emplacements. When the 27th Division entered the line, a general reshuffling of the XXIV Corps front took place, and Major-General Griner assumed responsibility for the extreme right flank of the corps. On the 16th, the 105th Infantry joined its parent unit after the fight for Tsugen Shima. All initial XXIV Corps deployments were completed by the 17th.

To the assault force leaders and their troops, the support provided for the attack by air, naval gunfire, and artillery was indeed awesome. The firepower of six battleships, six cruisers, and nine destroyers assigned to direct support of the attacking troops, and 650 Marine and Navy planes added to the lethal punch by hitting enemy defenses, assembly areas, and supply points.

Beginning at 0600 on the 19th, twenty-seven battalions of artillery, covering the Corps front with a density greater than one weapon to every thirty yards, fired in their pre-attack bombardment with everything from 75mm to 8-inch howitzers.

Equally impressive was the degree of air support offered the infantry, for at one time alone during 19th April, there were 375 aircraft on station, and LFASCU-2, 'controlling seven simultaneous strikes on a ten-mile front, had literally reached the point of saturation.' Commenting on this, Colonel Megee, the commander of the Marine LFASCUs, stated that he did 'not believe that we have ever exceeded or since equalled, this magnitude of close air support on any given day.'

To the troops poised for the attack, it was difficult to believe that any living thing could survive this awful rain of steel, yet it soon became apparent that almost all of the enemy did. They had hidden in caves and were protected by solid limestone walls deep within the hill-ridge complex astride the XXIV Corps route of advance. The assault infantry initially made some moderate gains, but when the Japanese remanned their positions, the attack slowed and then halted under the resumption of intense mortar, machine gun, and artillery fire that had been holding up the XXIV Corps attack prior to this date. Generally all along the line, gains were negligible to non-existent as enemy resistance stiffened.

Kakazu Ridge, now the objective of the 27th Division, proved as difficult to take as when the 96th Division had attempted this task. The fresh division mounted a battalion-sized infantry attack, supported by a reinforced tank company, in an attempt to bypass Kakazu Ridge by taking a cut running between the village of Kakazu and Nishibaru. Anticipating this maneuver, on 18th April the Japanese had emplaced mortars, machine guns, anti-tank guns, and antiaircraft cannon in position to cover the Ginowan-Shuri road, which crossed through the cut. Thus, the tank company was separated from its covering infantry as a result of the preplanned Japanese protective fires. Although the American armor was able to get behind the ridge to shoot up the village of Kakazu, without its supporting troops, the Shermans were forced to withdraw to their own lines. Only eight of the original thirty tanks in the force made it back through the cut. A combination of the deadly enemy fire and satchel charges placed by suicide-bent Japanese soldiers destroyed the remaining twenty-two.

By the end of the day, the 27th Division was halted at the western end of the Urasoe-Mura escarpment; the 96th Division, in the center of the corps line had pushed through Kaniku to gain positions on the forward slopes of Nishibaru Ridge; and the 7th Division on the left (east), was held up by fanatic opposition and heavy fire, resulting in no progress whatsoever. As the XXIV Corps began the second day of its offensive, the pattern of future fighting emerged – little yardage gained at high cost in lives to both sides. The action on this front during the period of 20th-24th April consisted of heavily supported local attacks against key enemy strongholds.

Frustrated in his initial attempts to breach the outer Shuri defenses, Hodges renewed the XXIV Corps attack on 24th April, ready to throw the full weight of every source of power he had at his disposal. Unknown to the Americans, however, and under the most intensive enemy artillery fire yet experienced on the Army front, during the night of 23rd-24th April, Ushijima had skilfully withdrawn his defending units from the line that had held up the 7th and 96th Division for two weeks. As a result, all along the front on the 24th, American forces were able to make sweeping and significant gains; even the heretofore-difficult Kakazu Ridge was taken with little effort.

Indications that greater Marine participation in the Shuri battle would soon be forthcoming occurred on 21st April when Tenth Army ordered Geiger to make the 1st Tank Battalion of the 1st Marine Division available to the 27th Infantry Division. Although the IIIAC commander was not unhappy about having his Marines take part in the fighting in the south, he was not too thrilled with the thought of having his forces committed piecemeal, perhaps to fight under an Army rather than a Marine commander. If Marines were needed in the southern front, then

the entire 1st Marine Division should be committed. Geiger's strong opinions in this matter apparently prevailed, for although a warning order had been issued for the disdisplacement south of the Marine tankers, it was never implemented. Instead, IIIAC was directed to designate a Marine division as Tenth Army reserve; Geiger selected de Valle's unit. One regiment was to be ready to assemble and move south on twelve hours' notice, and the 1st Marines was put on alert status.

It is appropriate to enquire at this point why the 2nd Marine Division, which was still part of the Iceberg force, fresh, and not yet involved in the fighting on Okinawa, was not committed on the island at a time when it became apparent that it was needed. On 9th April, Nimitz authorized the division to return to, and debark, at Saipan. Five days later the division was released from Tenth Army reserve and reverted to IIIAC control, although it remained on Saipan.

Both at this time, and in later critiques of the Okinawa campaign, considerable criticism arose from the fact that there was no sound reason why the 2nd Marine Division, a blooded and veteran fighting unit and expert in the conduct of amphibious assaults, could not have been employed to invade the southeastern coast of Okinawa at the Minatoga beaches. These were, after all, the alternate sites for Iceberg. Possibly, a second landing could have succeeded in drawing enough of the Japanese strength away from the Shuri defense line to permit it to be smashed much earlier than it actually was.

Even General Alexander A Vandegrift, Commandant of the Marine Corps, who was on Okinawa to see his Marines at this time, suggested the employment of the 2nd Division. In a meeting at Buckner's command post on 21st April, the matter was thrashed out, but the Tenth Army commander was unmoved in his belief that the greater need was for fresh troops on the Shuri front and

that a landing on the southeastern beaches was not feasible. Besides, in accordance with the Iceberg operation plan, the 2nd Division was scheduled to land on Kikai Jima – north of Okinawa – in July and he did not want to exhaust the unit before that time.

Facing up to the alternatives of mounting a two-corps frontal attack against Shuri or an envelopment of the Japanese lines over the southeastern beaches, Buckner decided against the latter and his next step, therefore, was to commit III Amphibious Corps in the south. The Marines became available to the Tenth Army when, on 26th April the Joint Chiefs of Staff cancelled Phase III of the Iceberg plan, which projected an invasion of Miyako Shima in the Sakishima Group east of Formosa. Commenting on this scheduled attack, Lieutenant-General Holland M Smith, the crusty and outspoken FMFPac commander, said that it was his 'opinion that the target is unnecessary – practically in a rear area and its capture will cost more than Iwo Jima.' Fortunately, his portents of doom were never put to the test. At any rate, IIIAC was freed from a future commitment and could be used immediately on Okinawa. Accordingly, on the 27th, the Tenth Army commander stated that he intended to relieve the 27th Infantry Division, which had been badly battered in the fighting for Kakazu, and to replace it with the 1st Marine Division. The former New York National Guard outfit was then assigned to garrison duty in the north under Island Command and slated to relieve the 6th Marine Division, which would then move to an assembly area in Chibana, prepared to move south and into the line. Also on 27th April, the 77th Division completed its move from Ie Shima to Okinawa and its leading elements moved into position to relieve the 96th Division the next day. Thus, the Tenth Army was ready to resume the attack with two fresh and rested divisions on line together with a relatively unchallenged 7th Division on the left flank and the 6th Division in reserve.

American redeployments and decisions followed close on the heels of

The commander visits his men:
General Vandergrift (right) arrives at
Yontan airfield on 20th April 1945

Supplies and ammunition for the Marines. When mud made communications difficult, the easiest delivery was by air (left)

one another as, on 28th April, Buckner informed IIIAC that the 1st Marine Division would relieve the 27th in two days and that on 7th May, Geiger's corps would take over the zone then held by the 1st Marine Division. Simultaneously, Tenth Army would assume tactical control of the two corps and would mount a coordinated army attack soon thereafter.

While preparations for the reliefs were underway, the XXIV Corps assault continued apace. The Japanese reacted savagely to the labored, grinding advance of the 96th Division towards its objective, the Maeda Escarpment. Thirty-second Army retention of this position was vitally important because, if the Americans took it, they would have a commanding view of all Japanese positions as far away as the Shuri foothills. Also in the present situation, the enemy had a direct line of sight into American lines. The region

surrounding Maeda, therefore, became the focal point of ferocious fighting as Ushijima's forces fought to the death to retain the dominating ground of the second Shuri defense ring. On 29th April, units of the 77th Division passed through the lines of the 96th and continued the attack. While the new division was somewhat fresher than the one it relieved, Bruce's men were nevertheless tired from the Ie Shima battle and the division overall was understrength. As a result, it could make only slight gains against the highly developed defenses.

Even before completing their relief of the 27th Division on 1st May, del Valle's Marines saw at first hand the nature of the fighting in southern Okinawa and soon learned of the tenacity of the enemy here. When the 5th Marines relieved the remaining Army regiments on the line that afternoon, it saw how hard these units had been hit. Each company of 2/5 relieved one depleted battalion of the 105th Infantry, and 3/5 took over in its entirety the area held by the 106th. At 1400, while consolidating their positions south of Awacha, 2/5

Marines observed about a platoon of Army tanks moving south in the town. As soon as the tanks had emerged from the town, they were hit by 47mm antitank fire within twenty yards of the Marine line. Even more disturbing to the Marines was the news that their unit identification and the location of their front had already been entered on an enemy map captured that day!

The first of May brought cloudy and cooler weather, and sporadic showers which gave warning of Okinawa's rainy period, which itself serves as a harbinger to the July-November typhoon season. On the next day, in driving rain and limited visibility which reduced the amount of air support available, the 1st Division began an attack to gain the northern bank of the Asa Gawa river. At the same time, the two XXIV Corps divisions attacked enemy-held ridge positions containing pillboxes and mutually supporting small arms and automatic weapons positions reinforced by fierce artillery fire. All forward movement resulted in only minimal gains these first days of May. As an indication of the ferocity of the fighting, by 2nd May, total 1st Marine Division casualties were fifty-four men killed, 233 wounded, and eleven missing – after only two days on the line. On the eastern flank of the XXIV Corps line, the 7th Division faced strong enemy positions, recently reinforced, in the Kochi area. For nearly two weeks, beginning about 23rd April, the 7th was held back by enemy positions emplaced on the many hills in the region, and all positions mutually supporting the others to frustrate the launching of a coordinated divisional attack. Here, as in so many of the other Japanese sectors on Okinawa, a thoroughly integrated defense line across the entire front concentrated such devastating fire against the Americans that they were denied any freedom of movement to maneuver into position for an effective attack. Ushijima's defensive concepts were proving successful beyond all his expectations.

The ferocity of Japanese resistance continued unabated all along the XXIV Corps front, for as veteran enemy units were annihilated, they were quickly rebuilt with fresh rear area troops or replaced with new infantry elements. Hodges' dire prediction at the beginning of the 19th April attack, that 'it is going to be really tough . . . and that I see no way to get (the Japanese) out except to blast them out yard by yard . . . ' was being all too grimly substantiated.

During the gruelling see-saw battle in the south, both sides paid a heavy price, but the enemy suffered to a greater extent. The brunt of the 19th April American attack was borne by the 62nd Division, and by the end of the month its strength had been cut in half. Although many of the Thirty-second Army officers had viewed their cause as hopeless from the very beginning of the American landings, they were buoyed up by the fact that after thirty consecutive days of fighting, the bulk of their forces remained

Right: Marine interpreter interrogates Japanese prisoner to gain vital intelligence. *Below:* Bazooka attack on a Japanese held ridge north of Naha

intact. Not yet committed in the fight for Shuri were most of the units of the 24th Division, the remainder of the 44th Independent Mixed Brigade, and the 5th Artillery Command, and the Naval Base Force. An attitude favoring the offense spread throughout Ushijima's command post, and a feeling that the commitment of these fresh troops in one fell swoop might very well blunt the American attack, if not, in fact, drive them off the island.

At this time, Ushijima decided that he no longer had any reason to fear an American landing in the southeastern area of the island. He therefore redeployed to positions in the Shuri defense area his forces previously immobilized in the Mintogawa region. In a week's time, by 27th April, the new defense reinforcements were sent in, but despite the infusion of these fresh troops in the front lines, small, local counterattacks failed. Steadily,

Destruction at Yontan airfield.
Below: Wreckage of Japanese planes.
Right: A bamboo dummy, built to decoy American fire-power

XXIV Corps troops pushed the enemy back and made incursions into his positions. Now, in the Japanese command post deep below Shuri Castle, Cho and other firebrands in the Thirty-second Army attempted to convince their commander that the time was ripe for an army-sized, all-out counterattack, with the relatively intact 24th Division as the spearhead.

Yahara, who had correctly predicted the fate of the mid-April counterattacks, was the lone dissenter this time also. He pointed out that the Americans were now positioned on commanding ground and that they were both numerically and materially superior. Yahara also reiterated the mission of the Thirty-second Army, and reasoned that it should 'maintain to the bitter end the principle of a strategic holding action.' Continuing on in this vein, he stated firmly that any other course of action would doom the army, change its mission, and open the way for an otherwise earlier invasion of the Japanese homeland.

Despite the reasoned and logical arguments of the army's operations

officer, the proponents of *guerre à outrance* swayed Ushijima to their way of thinking, and in the end prevailed. In scope and desired objectives, the attack plan was exceedingly ambitious – it called for nothing less than the complete destruction of XXIV Corps and the capture of Futema, mistakenly believed to be the headquarters of the Tenth Army.

This counterattack was to begin at 0500 (Y-Hour) on 5th May (X-Day), a time and date chosen because the Japanese believed that a relief of American lines was then taking place. According to the enemy attack plan, the 89th Regiment (on the right or east flank of the Japanese line) would penetrate the 7th Division lines to gain its objective, the Minami-Uebaru foothills, by sunset. In the center, the 22nd Regiment would hold its positions near Kochi and Onaga, where it would provide the assault units with fire support. When the 89th Regiment established an east-west line at Tanabaru, the first phase objective, the 22nd would move out, destroying all American units to its front and follow in the traces of

the 32nd Regiment, which was to make the main division effort in the center. At Y-Hour, the 32nd would drive forward to seize 77th Division's positions southeast of Maeda, and then continue on to gain the heights west of Tanabaru, also by sunset.

After it had moved from positions near Ishimmi to penetrate the 77th Division lines west of Kochi, the 27th Tank Regiment would furnish armored support to the attack, and then take up positions to assist both the 22nd and 32nd Regiments. Further west, on the left of the Japanese line, the 44th IMB was to move to an area northwest of Shuri, where it would provide security on the left flank until the initial objective was taken. Immediately thereafter, it would swing north to Oyama and the coast just beyond to isolate the 1st Marine Division from the scene of the major fighting. Supporting this effort was the heretofore uncommitted 62nd Division. To ensure that the Marines would be cut off, Japanese planners had reinforced the 44th IMB with considerable armor, artillery, and anti-tank strength. On the night of 3rd-

4th May, the guns, mortars, and howitzers of the 5th Artillery Command were to move out of their hidden positions into the open to provide the attack with massive artillery support. Ota's naval elements were also to be brought into play, for he was directed to form four infantry battalions from his command to be used as army reserve in exploiting the anticipated breakthrough.

Japanese planners also made provision to hit the open flanks of the Tenth Army. A makeshift navy of landing barges, small craft, native canoes, and other spitkits would embark from Naha on the night of 3rd-4th May and land a major portion of the 26th Shipping Engineer Regiment behind 1st Marine Division lines at Oyama. At the same time, elements of the 26th, 28th and 29th Sea Raiding squadrons were to wade the reef on the Marine flank, go ashore in the vicinity of Kuwan, and move inland to support the counterlanding of the 26th Regiment. Committed to this coastal attack were approximately 700 men.

The envelopment on the east coast was to be conducted by about 500 men of the 23rd Shipping Engineer Regiment and the 27th Sea Raiding Squadron landing behind the 7th Division at Tsuwa. The mission of both enveloping units was to infiltrate American rear areas in small groups and to destroy equipment and harass CPs with grenades and demolitions. No concerted attacks were to be made by groups of less than one hundred men. If all went according to plan, the two counterlanding elements would join up near the center of the island to assist the advance of the 24th Division.

A never-changing assumption in Iceberg intelligence estimates was that the enemy had the capability of mounting a large-scale counterattack. As of the evening of 3rd May, however, an analysis of recent Japanese action indicated that the enemy was more likely to continue fighting a series of delaying actions from successive positions, defending each one until annihilated. Since the American's enemy order of battle file was relatively current and indications of an imminent major attack were

not perceptible, none was really expected. XXIV Corps troops were not caught offguard, however, when the attack was finally mounted.

Preceding the two-day struggle, which Yahara later called 'the decisive action of the campaign,' was the fifth mass *Kamikaze* attack, which struck at dusk on 3rd May. It was mounted specifically by the Fifth Air Fleet to support the Thirty-second Army effort. Although they were to play a secondary role in the counterattack, the *Kamikaze* pilots wrought greater destruction and were more successful in their effort than the Japanese ground forces. Of the 159 planes participating in the attack, thirty-six were shot down within two hours of their appearance over Okinawa. While the conventional bombers were forced to remain at great heights over the island because of the curtain of antiaircraft fire, the suiciders were able to bore in on the transport area and the radar picket craft to inflict wide-spread damage. Before the first phase of the air attack had ended, a destroyer and an LSM were sunk and two minelayers and an LCS put out of commission. Beginning at 0600 on 4th May, and for four hours thereafter, the *Kamikazes* renewed their murderous onslaught against the radar pickets. By the time that the morning forays, and another one at dusk were over, the number of naval casualties and ships damaged was sobering. There were ninety-one sailors killed, 280 wounded, and 283 missing in this attack. And on the picket line, two more destroyers, a minesweeper, a light minelayer, and an LCS were damaged. In the morning attack, a suicider hit a turret on the cruiser *Birmingham*, and in the afternoon attack another enemy pilot succeeded in crashing the flight deck of the carrier *Sangamon*, causing an explosion which damaged both elevators and destroyed twenty-one planes.

American surface forces as well as carrier and land-based planes were involved in thwarting the enemy effort. The screens of cruisers, destroyers, and gunboats on both coasts were warned to be alert to a threat from the Sea Raiding Squadrons. As a result, these screens discovered

the Shipping Engineer Regiments attempting to slip behind American lines and the naval elements assisted the ground forces in fighting off the counterlandings by illuminating and shelling the enemy. When the extent of the Japanese ground effort was discovered after dawn on 4th May, two battleships, five cruisers, and eight destroyers assigned as XXIV Corps' daylight gunfire support joined with artillery and air in pushing the enemy back.

A steadily accelerating rate of artillery fire, falling mainly on the front lines of the 7th and 77th Divisions, began the Japanese counteroffensive after dark of 3rd May. As American guns replied in kind, the normal battlefield din became an almost unbearable cacophony. In a comparatively less noisy sector near Machinato airfield, armored amphibian tractor crews on guard at the coast opened up on unidentified individuals they heard on the beach. Shortly thereafter, they saw naval support craft firing at targets in the water just off shore. Less than an hour after this outbreak of firing, the 1st Marines reported enemy barges heading in for shore at Kuwan.

The enemy landing took place here rather than at Oyama, as originally planned, because the landing craft carrying the bulk of the attack force had trouble negotiating the route through the reefs and lost the way. The Japanese added to their woes by attempting to land at the very point where a reinforced Marine rifle com-

Another victim of *Kamikaze* attack among the anchored fleet

pany had anchored its defenses for the night.

The stealthy enemy approach went undetected by beach sentries and became known only when a clamorous babble signalled the opening of the attack. This alert resulted in an immediate response from the Marines. They quickly fired their previously registered machine guns and mortars on the overcrowded barges. A combination of burning barges, flares, and tracers soon gave the battle scene a surrealistic glow. The illumination of the reef revealed Japanese heads bobbing in the water and provided the Marine riflemen and machine gunners with targets which they unmercifully raked with heavy fire, and thus blunted the enemy attempt at enveloping the west coast. By dawn of 4th May, the Japanese remnants at Kuwan were almost completely mopped up.

Other enemy landings were attempted before dawn behind 1st Marine Division lines further up the west coast. Most of these efforts were doomed to failure when the combined fires of naval vessels, armored amtracs, infantry, and service troops destroyed the boats when still offshore, or when, by the light of day, the few Japanese able to reach shore were hunted down with the help of scout and sentry dogs, and killed. On the east coast, the counterlanding met with the same spectacular lack

Above: Flame throwing tank in action at Coral Ridge. *Left:* Infantry move in to clear a fiercely defended draw

of success, for the American naval screen and the 7th Division cut the shipping engineers to pieces, killing an estimated 700. Thus, the Thirty-second Army gambit failed, and there was little indication that the rest of Ushijima's counterattack plan could be fulfilled.

The artillery fire supporting the main enemy ground attack reached a crescendo at about 0430 on 4th May, when thousands of mortar projectiles fell on American front lines as the attackers attempted to breach XXIV Corps defenses. Japanese assault units suffered equally from their own fire as well as from American concentrations as they moved under the rolling barrages supporting their attack. The enemy attempt was thoroughly blunted, however, by a blanket of steel laid down by naval gunfire, air, and sixteen battalions of divisional artillery, reinforced by twelve battalions of 155mm guns and 155mm and 8-inch howitzers from XXIV Corps Artillery.

Beginning at daybreak on the 4th, the first of 134 planes to fly support for XXIV Corps made its initial bombing run. By 1900, American planes had expended seventy-seven tons of bombs, 450 rockets, and 22,000 rounds of machine gun and 20mm cannon ammunition on Japanese troop concentrations and artillery positions. Even in face of the *Kamikaze* attacks, gunfire support vessels, ranging from battleships to patrol and landing craft, ranged the coastal waters delivering observed and call fire on enemy targets.

The heavy smoke which the Thirty-second Army had ordered placed on Tenth Army lines obscured the enemy's view of the progress of the battle as they observed it from the Shuri heights. Despite the fact that it was a blatant lie, good news telling of the success of the 24th Division's offensive poured into the Thirty-second Army command post shortly after the attack began.

All along the line the Japanese efforts failed abjectly. Darkness of 4th May found the Tenth Army in firm control of the real estate it had held when the enemy attack began. Not only had XXIV Corps troops firmly held their original positions, but in some cases, even in the face of withering Japanese fire and the momentum of an attacking force, the Americans had counterattacked and actually gained new enemy territory.

As darkness fell on the 4th, its gloom was no deeper than that already pervading the Thirty-second Army command post. As the shambles of the crushed counterattack were surveyed by Ushijima's staff, it became quite apparent that it had been a failure. The next day, all along the XXIV Corps line, American troops hunted down the survivors of the initial enemy push. In the course of this day's action, the 1st Marine Division gained the banks of the Asa Kawa, and began digging in on the commanding ground overlooking the river line to await a new counterattack that never came.

Following these two days of battle, Tenth Army casualty figures showed that the 7th and 77th Divisions, which had felt the full fury of the Japanese attack, lost a total of 714 soldiers killed, wounded, and missing in action. The 1st Marine Division, which had continued its drive to the

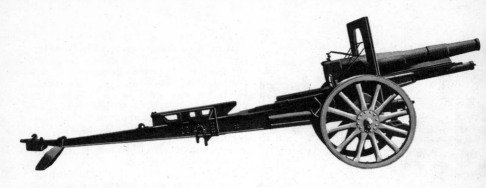

The 155mm howitzer (Japan)
Properly known as the Model 4 (1915), the Japanese 155mm howitzer was an old weapon. The later Model 96 (1936) could be elevated to the unusually high angle of 75° if a pit were dug below the breech to enable the howitzer to be loaded at this angle. The Model 4 weighed 6,100 lbs in action and had a maximum range of 10,500 yards

south during the enemy effort, suffered a total of 649 casualties. Reflecting the fury with which the Japanese had fought and the punishment they had sustained, enemy losses – that is, the number of bodies actually counted in front of XXIV Corps lines – totalled 6,237 men, almost all of whom were irreplaceable veterans. This figure must be considered low, for the Japanese undoubtedly retrieved some of their dead and evacuated some wounded, who died later.

Checked by the tremendous fire power of the Tenth Army, each Japanese division in the attack lost approximately seventy-five percent of its original strength; enemy artillery personnel strength was halved, and fifty-nine artillery pieces were completely destroyed. Following this time, never again in the Okinawa battle did Tenth Army troops receive such intensively destructive Japanese artillery fire as that which preceded the counterattack. The net result of this doomed effort was that the Thirty-second Army was compelled to abandon the offensive on the night of 5th May and to return to its old positions and defensive posture.

As he had anticipated, Yahara's dire predictions were realized, and he won a tearful promise from Ushijima that his counsel would be followed in the future. Japanese tactics were revised to consist of holding actions in previously prepared and

strongly fortified positions. Again, the Americans would be forced to advance in the face of withering small arms, automatic weapons, and mortar fire. The final judgement on the worth of the counterattack was given by its strongest proponent, Cho, who, according to a reliable report, 'abandoned all hope of a successful outcome of the operation and declared that only time intervened between defeat and the 32nd Army.'

On 5th May, Buckner ordered the attack to the south continued with two corps abreast; IIIAC on the right and XXIV Corps on the left. The 1st Marine Division would revert to parent control on the 7th, and the attack that day was to be a prelude to a second and major assault to be launched four days later. The 6th Marine Division was to take over the right (coastal) flank of the corps zone on 8th May.

In front of the 1st Marine Division was a strongly held enemy line which ran roughly from Jichaku and Uchima through the ridges north of Dakeshi and Awacha. Frontal and flanking fire from the well-organized maze protecting Dakeshi poured down on the Marine attackers as they attempted to advance on 6th May in rainy weather which lasted for two days. The attempt to breach the Dakeshi defenses was unavailing, and even a four-battalion artillery preparation as well as air and naval gunfire bombardments on the Awacha

Pocket didn't permit the 5th Marines to gain more than a few yards. By the morning of the 7th, it became apparent that a deep draw in front of this regiment's positions contained the bulk of the enemy's Awacha defenses. Del Valle and the regimental commander, Colonel John H Griebel, decided to begin the attack on Awacha at noon, following an extensive air, artillery, and rocket preparation, and to support the infantry with a reinforced tank company.

The fighting that afternoon was marked by tactics which 'General Buckner, with an apt sense of metaphor, called . . . the "blowtorch and corkscrew" method. Liquid flame was the blowtorch; explosives, the corkscrew.' Marine flamethrower and demolition teams burnt out and sealed many of the enemy cave installations in their zone, and by 1700, when the attack was halted for the night, the resultant gains were slight. Even though enemy troops gave way slightly during the day, it was obvious that Awacha Pocket was not going to be taken quickly or easily.

News of the collapse of Nazi Germany and the declaration of V-E Day on 8th May drew little response of any sort from either side on Okinawa. Most of the cold, rain-soaked Americans and Japanese in the front lines were concerned only with that very small but vital part of the war where their own lives were at stake. Still, V-E Day did not go unnoticed at Okinawa. The Iceberg forces conducted Thanksgiving services on board many of the ships in the anchorage, and, in addition, the voices of naval gunfire and field artillery helped in the celebration. At exactly noon, every available fire support ship directed a full-gun salvo at the enemy, and three battalions of IIIAC Artillery massed their fires on a suspected Japanese CP. The results of the noontime shoot were not determined, but, in the words of one observer, 'it made one hell of a big noise.'

During 9th and 10th May, the 6th Division moved up to the Asa Kawa and prepared to cross it. This river crossing was only a part of the all-out army attack scheduled for the 11th. Envisioned in the objectives of this plan were the envelopment and destruction of Japanese forces holding the Shuri bastion, and the total annihilation of Ushijima's command.

As conceived in Tenth Army plans, the object of the full-scale attack beginning on 11th May was to destroy the defenses guarding Shuri. In the end, this massive assault took the lives of thousands of men in two weeks of the bloodiest fighting experienced during the entire Okinawa campaign. For each front line division, the struggle to overcome enemy troops on the major terrain feature in the path of its advance determined the nature of the battle. Facing the front of the 96th Division was Conical Hill; the 77th Division fought for Shuri itself. Marines of the 1st Division had to overcome Wana Draw, while Sugar Loaf Hill was the objective facing the 6th Division.

Heavy rains and the resultant muddy terrain seriously began to affect the American offensive and restricted the amount of air support which could operate under these conditions. Again following a softening-up preparation by supporting arms, at noon on the 9th, the 5th Marines, reinforced by a battalion of the 7th Marines, attacked the mouth of Awacha Draw. Initially the attack was successful and moved ahead rapidly, but flanking fire enfiladed the lines and held up the Marine advance. During the night of 9th-10th May, the Japanese made numerous infiltration attempts in the 1st Marine Division zone, but were beaten off, as were two enemy counterattacks in which the attackers had closed to bayonet range. Despite these slight harassments, the attack against Awacha continued at 0800 on the 10th.

The most violent enemy reaction came from positions centered around Dakeshi Ridge and the high ground to the east along the corps boundary. Less than an hour after the attack began, 1/5 was pinned down by heavy enemy fire that skyrocketed casualty figures. Nonetheless, the remaining two battalions made inroads into enemy positions. With artillery and flamethrower tanks supporting, 2/5 overran all enemy resistance to its front and advanced into the heart of the Awacha defenses. Many enemy

pockets of resistance were bypassed, however, and had to be cleaned out after all of Awacha had been taken on the 11th.

Meanhile, the 7th Marines had been tasked with the mission of clearing the Japanese from Dakeshi, which lay in the path of the American advance. Beginning 10th May, the regiment, reinforced with a battalion from the 5th Marines, jumped off with two rifle battalions in the assault and two in reserve. The right battalion was immobilized at the line of departure by accurate mortar and artillery shelling, as well as by heavy small arms fire coming from pillboxes and caves to its front. Despite this steel barrier, the troops slowly advanced and made some headway, only to relinquish this ground at the end of the day because the newly captured real estate was untenable. To the right of the division line, the other assault regiment – the 1st Marines – attempted to gain the road leading west out of Dakeshi. By 1600 on the 10th, leading infantry elements reached a small ridge overlooking the road, but extremely heavy machine gun fire from Dakeshi Ridge – in front of the 7th Marines – prevented further forward movement, and it became painfully clear that no advance could be made until the ridge had been taken.

On 11th May, the 7th Marines relentlessly resumed the attack on Dakeshi. The infantry moved forward in the face of Japanese mortars, grenades, and, from pillboxes and coral caves, automatic weapons fire. By 1800, the attack was halted on positions then held on the ridge overlooking and running through Dakeshi. As the men of 2/7 dug in for the night, some of the veterans of the Peleliu campaign were reminded of how much the fight for the ridge that day resembled the action at Bloody Nose Ridge, whose name is most descriptive of the type of action they experienced there in September 1944. Throughout the night of 11th-12th May, the new tenants on Dakeshi Ridge fought off numerous infiltra-

Above: Harassing night fire directed at Japanese positions. *Below:* Marines battle for ridge

tion attempts by its previous residents, who attacked under the cover of continuous artillery and mortar barrages coming from emplacements on Wana Ridge.

The fall of aggressively defended and vital Dakeshi Ridge, and its occupation by the Marines, meant that one more barrier to the heart of the Shuri defenses had been razed. In addition, the Japanese were now denied the use of commanding ground from which the terrain from Shuri and Naha to Machinato Ridge –. and the entire coastal area in between – could be covered by observation and fire. The capture of Dakeshi Ridge decisively and effectively breached the enemy's Naha-Shuri-Yonabaru line and raised doubts about how much longer the Thirty-second Army could hold it before Shuri itself was threatened. Dakeshi village was taken and cleared on the 13th.

During the fighting for Awacha Pocket and Dakeshi, the 6th Division to the right of the 1st and on the west coast flank of the Tenth Army, pushed a footbridge across the Awa Kawa on 10th May and established a bridgehead on the south bank of the river, which came under immediate enemy artillery fire. During the night of 10th-11th May, a Bailey bridge was constructed permitting a strong force of armor-supported infantry to cross the river and to join in the coordinated two-corps Tenth Army attack.

The major effort in the XXIV Corps zone was mounted by the 96th Division, left of the center of the line. While the 77th Division pressured the enemy through central Okinawa towards Shuri, the 96th – which had relieved the 7th Division on 10th May – approached a hill mass directly northwest of Yonabaru. This terrain feature controlled the eastern reaches to Shuri, completely dominated the east-central coastal plain, and was the easternmost anchor of the Thirty-second Army's main battle position. All natural routes to Conical Hill, as this stronghold was aptly named, were constantly under observation and thoroughly covered by Japanese fire.

Conical Hill commanded a series of ridges and other lesser hills, whose capture was to be costly and time-consuming. Murderous fire during the 11th May attack forced 96th Division front-line units to relinquish whatever gains had been made that day. At the same time, 77th Division assault battalions could only advance 400–500 yards against a strongly entrenched enemy, who took advantage of the broken terrain to take the flanks, and at times the rear, of the advancing infantry under fire. On the 12th, 96th Division assault elements executed a flanking maneuver west of Conical to gain a foothold from which the stronghold could be re-

Right: Troops with flame throwers advance on Shuri, shielded by tanks
Below: Flame throwing and artillery firing tanks neutralize a pocket

duced. The division captured the western and northern slopes the next day and thus opened the way for the capture of Yonabaru and at the same time unlocked another door leading to Shuri's inner defenses.

On the opposite coast, the 6th Marine Division moved out in face of small arms fire pouring down from positions in rocky cliffs overlooking its route of advance and from the mouths of Okinawan tombs dug in the hillsides that lined it. By 0920, Shepherd's Marines reached the high ground commanding a view of Naha below, and sent out patrols through the suburbs of the city to the banks of the Asato Gawa.

While the ground fighting went on unabated, the war in the air continued with neither side giving quarter. The fifth mass *Kamikaze* raid of the campaign occurred on 10th-11th May, unintentionally prefacing the Tenth Army ground attack on the 11th. Most of the enemy sorties heading for Okinawa on the 10th were kept well away from the island and American shipping offshore. This situation changed radically the next day, when, at 0630, TAF pilots intercepted the first in a series of suiciders attempting to crash targets in the Ie Shima and Hagushi anchorages. Successful as the alert American combat air patrols were in protecting assault shipping and the radar picket vessels, it was impossible to prevent losses as long as even a single Japanese plane penetrated the Iceberg air screen. In at least five instances in May, *Kamikazes* that had been so seriously damaged in air-to-air combat that they could not have possible returned to home bases – and conceivably could not have even recovered level flight – managed to remain on course, penetrate the air screen and ships' AA fire, and hit their targets.

After dark on 17th May, the range of Tenth Army air operations was extended to Japan for the first time since L-Day. On that evening, a pair of P-47 Thunderbolts from the AAFs 318th Fighter Group on Ie Shima rocketed and strafed three airfields on southern Kyushu during this first long-range TAF mission. Adding insult to injury, the Army pilots strafed

the brightly lit streets of Kanoya before returning home unchallenged by Japanese flyers. If nothing else, this raid on Kyushu demonstrated the complete ascendancy of American air power in an area which, to this time, had been solely the province of Japanese aviators. This evidence of American and British air strength – for planes of Rawlings British Carrier Force were also active in the air over the East China Sea – did not, however, convince the Japanese that continuation of the mass *Kamikaze* raids was merely an exercise in futility.

American planes rising from now-crowded strips on Yontan, Kadena, and Ie Shima fields successfully smashed the suicide attacks, and as a result, Special Attack Force aircraft and pilot losses mounted out of all proportion to the results achieved. Imperial General Headquarters then decided that the only way to reverse the situation was to destroy Iceberg planes on the ground at their Okinawa bases. A surprise ground attack mission was then assigned to the *Giretsu* (Act of Heroism) Airborne Raiding Force. Armed with demolition charges, grenades, and light arms, the commandos were ordered to land on Kadena and Yontan fields and to make one desperate attempt to destroy aircraft, facilities, and personnel and thus cripple American air operations. The planes carrying the group were to accompany those in the formation of *Kikusui* number 7.

Left : Japanese gun concealed in cave is now silent
Above and below : Eight days of Okinawan rain generate problems in the field

Above and below: Japanese bodies and wreckage litter the Yontan field after desperate commando raid. *Right:* Aftermath of *Kamikaze* attack

The 120-man suicide force, divided into five platoons and a command section, was flown to the target in twelve twin-engine bombers. At about 2000 on 24th May, Yontan and Kadena airfields were bombed as a prelude to the airborne raid. Approximately two and a half hours later, Yontan-based antiaircraft artillerymen and aviation personnel were startled to see several Japanese bombers rashly but purposely attempting to land. With one exception, the planes that were shot down over the field either attempted to crash ground facilities and parked aircraft or went plummeting down in flames, carrying their entrapped troops with them.

The one plane that was not shot down managed to make a wheels-up landing, and before it had even skidded to a stop, the raiders poured out, began throwing grenades and explosive charges at the nearest parked airplanes, and then sprayed the area with small arms fire. The confusion which followed this almost unbelievable event is hard to recount, for much is lost in the telling. Uncontrolled American rifle and machine gun fire laced the airfield and vicinity, and probably caused most of the Iceberg casualties.

When the attack was over, sixty-nine Japanese dead were counted and there were no prisoners. Although they disrupted airfield operations for only a short time, the raiders managed to destroy eight planes, damage twenty-four others, and set fire to the fuel dumps, causing the loss of 70,000 gallons of precious aviation gasoline before the fires were extinguished.

Meanwhile, as this ground foray unfolded, approximately 445 planes – of which nearly one-third were suiciders – struck at shipping, concentrating again on the radar pickets. The first phase of this attack broke off at about 0300 on the 25th, only to resume at dawn with a frenzy that continued during the day. Shipping losses and naval casualties were once more heavy.

The last *Kamikaze* raid of May began just two days later, on the 27th, and lasted until the evening of the 28th. Heavy antiaircraft fire and combat air patrols fought off the invaders, but not before a destroyer had been sunk and eleven other ships damaged to varying degrees. By the end of May, Air Defense Command pilots had added 279-1/4 claimed kills to their April figures, giving TAF a total of 423 enemy planes destroyed in the air during fifty-six days of operations. In this same period, 7th April through 31st May, only three American planes were shot down out of the 109 aircraft lost to such other causes as pilot error, aircraft malfunctions, and cases of mistaken identity by friendly AAA units. Although the weather during most of May limited air operations, both sides flew a number of missions despite minimal flying conditions. By the middle of May, TAF had reached the state where it was fully prepared to provide the fullest possible support to Tenth Army troops, then poised to strike at the heart of the Shuri defenses.

Reduction of the Shuri barrier

All Tenth Army front line units jumped off in the attack at 0730 on 14th May. Their primary objectives were to clear the eastern and western approaches to Shuri and to envelope the strongly defended flanks of that bastion. Especially bitter fighting was experienced in the Marine zone, where the 1st and 6th Divisions unsuccessfully attempted to break through the defenses west of Wana and northwest of Naha; these appeared to be the main Japanese line of resistance. This assumption was proved correct during the course of the attack by the heavy losses sustained by attacking infantry units and the eighteen 1st and 6th Tank Battalion Shermans damaged and destroyed by enemy antitank, mortar,

and artillery fire as well as by mines and suicide attacks of individual Japanese soldiers.

The 6th Marine Division moved forward with two rifle regiments on line – the 22nd Marines on the left and the 29th Marines on the right along the west coast. The heaviest fighting of the day was experienced on the extreme left flank of the 22nd Marines, where the 2nd Battalion ran into a system of strongly defended and thoroughly organized defenses. These positions guarded a rectangularly shaped, dominating, and precipitous hill that was quickly dubbed 'Sugar Loaf.' A concentration of power here had easily blunted the attacks of 2/22 in the previous two days. Japanese dispositions on Sugar Loaf were so organized that the defenders could cover the front, rear, and flanks of any portion of the position with interlocking bands of automatic weapons fire and devastating barrages from mortars, artillery, and grenade launchers – more popularly, but incorrectly, called knee mortars.

Although the intensity of Japanese resistance increased proportionally as assault troops approached nearer, it was not realized at first that this bristling stronghold and its environs constituted the western anchor of the Shuri defenses. At the time that the 22nd Marines reached Sugar Loaf, the regimental line was spread out and overextended, and excessive casualties during the approach to the enemy position had reduced the combat efficiency of the regiment to approximately sixty-two percent.

Despite this situation, at 1500 on the 14th, Shepherd ordered 2/22 to seize, occupy, and defend the battalion objective – including Sugar Loaf – at any cost this day. Reinforced by another infantry company, the battalion moved out at 1722 behind a line of tanks and an artillery-laid smoke screen. This was the second time on the 14th that Company F, the lead element, had attacked Sugar Loaf. Slightly more than two hours later, some forty survivors of two rifle companies – each numbering 242 men at full strength – were digging for cover at the foot of the hill under the com-

115

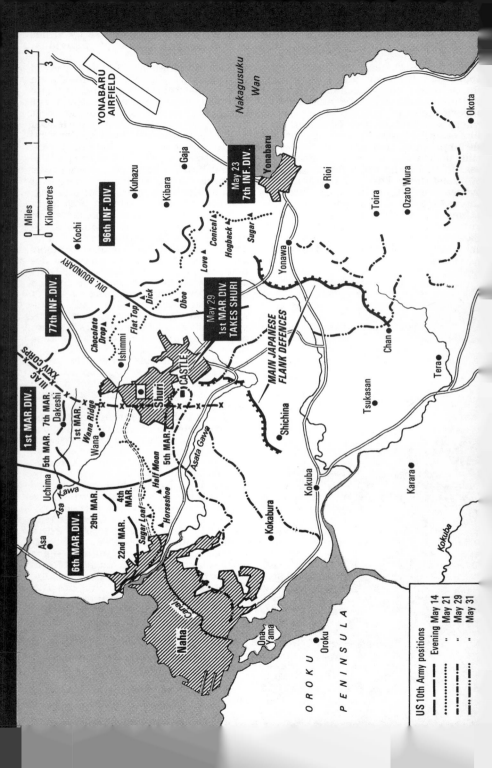

mand of the battalion executive officer, Major Henry A Courtney, Jr.

Japanese snipers appeared to be firing from all directions at this lonely group of Marines, who were also taken under enemy mortar fire from the flanks as well as the reverse slopes of Sugar Loaf. To carry supplies and much-needed ammunition to the exposed men and to reinforce the pitifully small force, the battalion commander sent twenty-six newly arrived replacements forward. All during their dash to the Courtney group, the Japanese were rolling grenades down on the Marine position from the heights above, leaving Major Courtney no alternative but to attack up the hill to seize its crest. At 2300, all American illumination of the area ceased, and the major led his small force up the hill, all throwing grenades as they charged. As soon as the Marines carried the crest, they dug in to wait out a night of anticipated counterattacks and the customarily heavy enemy mortar fire generally experienced on a newly won position.

Sugar Loaf Hill was but one of three enemy positions in a triaangularly shaped group of hills which made up the western anchor of the Shuri defense system. Sugar Loaf was the apex of the triangle and faced north. Its flanks and rear were well covered by extensive cave and tunnel positions in Half Moon Hill to the southeast and the Horseshoe to the southwest. The three elements of this system were mutually supporting. A sharp depression in the Horseshoe afforded the enemy mortar positions that were almost inaccesible to any supporting arm short of direct, aimed rifle fire and hand grenades. Any attempt to capture Sugar Loaf by flanking action from the east to west was immediately exposed to flat trajectory fire from supporting positions on both of the other two terrain features. Likewise, an attempt to reduce either the Horseshoe or Half Moon would be exposed to destructive, well-aimed fire from Sugar Loaf.

In addition, the three bastions were connected by a network of tunnels and galleries which made reinforcement an easy matter for the enemy.

As a final factor in the strength of Sugar Loaf, all sides of the hill were precipitous and there were no evident avenues of approach into the hill mass itself. As the 6th Division commander pointed out in his report following the Okinawa campaign, 'For strategic location and tactical strength, it is hard to conceive of a more powerful position than the Sugar Loaf terrain afforded. Added to all the foregoing was the bitter fact that troops assaulting this position presented a clear target to enemy machine guns, mortars, and artillery emplaced on the Shuri heights to their left and left rear.'

This, then, was the position that Courtney and his small band held for the time being. Shortly after they had reached the top and dug in, enemy fire fell on them and increased in intensity almost immediately, to be followed by the first in a series of anticipated counterattacks to regain the hill. Shortly after midnight of 14th-15th May, sounds of enemy activity on the reverse slope of the crest signified an impending *Banzai* attack. To forestall this charge, Courtney led his men in a grenade-throwing charge of his own against the reverse-slope defenders, and was killed during this action. For his bravery and outstanding leadership in this night's action, Courtney joined that small group of heroes on Okinawa – and other American campaigns – decorated with his country's highest award, the Medal of Honor. And like many of those individuals similarly decorated, his, too, was a posthumous award.

By dawn, only twenty-five Marines of Courtney's original group and a reinforcing rifle company were on the hill, and they faced still another enemy counterattack. At 1136, the few survivors were pulled from the position to man a hastily organized defense line set up on the high ground just in front of Sugar Loaf. The counterattack was just the beginning of a series of such attacks which soon reached battalion-sized proportions and spread over a 900-yard front extending into the zones of adjacent units. Although an intensive air, naval gunfire, and artillery preparation scheduled for the division assault that morning slowed the attackers, their frenzy remained unabated and the momentum of their counterattack unchecked. By 1315, however, the Japanese effort was spent, though not before the center of the 22nd Marines had taken a terrific pounding.

To forestall further enemy counterattacks expected to be mounted in this area, two rifle companies were ordered to seize blocking positions on a hill northwest of Sugar Loaf. Meanwhile, the 29th Marines was directed to take Half Moon Hill on the 15th. In the van of the attack, the 1st and 3rd Battalions experienced the same bitter and costly resistance encountered by the 22nd Marines. A slowly paced advance was made under constant harassing fire from the Shuri heights area. By late afternoon, 1/29 reached a valley north of Half Moon and immediately became engaged in a grenade-throwing duel with defenders on the reverse slopes of the hill. Armor supporting the Marine assault elements came under direct 150mm howitzer fire at this point.

The success of the 6th Division attack on the 16th depended upon the capture of Half Moon by the 29th Marines. Once 3/29 had seized the high ground east of Sugar Loaf, 3/22 was to mount the major division effort and capture the hill fortress itself. This attack was to no avail and the assault forces had to withdraw to that morning's jumping off point to set up night defenses. The northern slope of Half Moon was occupied by 3/29 against slight resistance, but at 1500 the picture changed drastically when the Japanese mounted a massive counterattack supported by heavy fire from all of their supporting weapons. As evening approached, the increasing enemy

fire forced the Marines to withdraw to their original lines, where they set in a perimeter defense for the night.

The 16th May was categorized by the 6th Division as the bitterest of the Okinawa campaign, a day when 'the regiments had attacked with all the effort at their command and had been unsuccessful.' The 22nd Marines had been so sorely punished in the fighting, that the regimental commander reported the combat efficiency of his unit was down to forty percent. Recognizing that the fighting of the preceding eight days had sapped the vitality and offensive capabilities of the 22nd Marines to a point where it was inadvisable to continue its employment in the attack, Shepherd shifted boundaries to place Sugar Loaf in the zone of the 29th Marines. Thus, this regiment was made responsible for the seizure of both this hill and Half Moon. While

the mission seemed insurmountable, it appeared that, in this case at least, fewer problems of control would arise if one unit directed the attack on the two objectives.

To neutralize the seemingly impregnable enemy defenses in front of the 29th Marines, the attack of 17th May was preceded by an intensive bombardment of all regimental objectives. Included in this massive preparation were the fires of 16-inch naval rifles, 8-inch howitzers, and 1,000-pound bombs. Following this softening-up treatment and spearheaded by a heavy and continual artillery barrage, the 29th Marines launched a tank-infantry attack with three battalions abreast. Like previous efforts, this one was thwarted also, even though Company E of 2/29 gained the top of Sugar Loaf and held, despite a Japanese counterattack. Heavy casualties and a depleted ammunition supply forced the battalion commander to withdraw the survivors of the company from Sugar Loaf. Thus, the prize for which 160 Marines of Company E had been killed and wounded on that day was returned to the enemy.

So well integrated were the enemy defenses on Half Moon, Horseshoe, and Sugar Loaf that capture of only one position was meaningless; the 6th Division had to take at least two of them simultaneously. If only one hill was seized without the others being neutralized or similarly captured, effective Japanese fire from the uncaptured positions would force the Marines to withdraw from the other two. This, in effect, was why Sugar Loaf had not been breached before this, and why it was not taken on the 17th.

On 18th May at 0946, less than an hour after the 29th Marines attacked, Sugar Loaf was again occupied by 6th Division troops. The assault began with Marine armor attempting a double envelopment of the hill with little initial success, and the loss of six tanks. Despite this setback and increasingly accurate artillery fire, a company of the mediums split

Flame thrower tank in action against Japanese stronghold on one of the Shuri hills

up and managed to reach and occupy positions on either flank of Sugar Loaf from which they could cover the reverse slopes of the hill. Shortly thereafter, infantry elements overran the crest of the hill and pushed down its south slope to mop up and destroy enemy emplacements there.

All during this day's attacks on Sugar Loaf and Half Moon, the enemy on Horseshoe Hill poured down a never-ending rain of mortar and machine gun fire on the Marines below. To destroy these emplacements, a rifle company was committed to them while other Marines on its flank and those on Sugar Loaf supported it by fire. The assault unit pressed forward to the ridge marking the lip of the Horseshoe ravine, only to be stopped by a vicious mortar and hand-grenade barrage coming from the deeply entrenched enemy. Because of this intense fire, the Marines withdrew slightly to the forward slope of the ridge where it set in a defense for the night.

The coming of darkness on the 18th was not accompanied by any noticeable waning in the furious contest for possession of Sugar Loaf, a battle in which the combat efficiency of the 29th Marines, like its sister regiment, the 22nd, was sorely tried, but not found wanting. Nevertheless, in the nearly nine days since the Tenth Army had first begun its major push, the 6th Marine Division sustained 2,662 battle and 1,289 non-battle casualties, almost all occurring in the ranks of the 22nd and 29th Marines. It was patently obvious that an infusion of fresh blood into the division line was a prerequisite if the attack was to be continued with undiminshed fervor. Therefore, on 19th May, the 4th Marines was released from IIIAC reserve and entered the lines, relieving the 29th Marines. It received its baptism of fire in the south while attacking the Sugar Loaf complex.

Preceded by a thorough artillery preparation and supported by the 6th Tank Battalion, the 5th Provisional Rocket Detachment, and the Army 91st Chemical Company (firing 4.2-inch mortars), the 4th Marines attacked Half Moon and Horseshoe Hills. By the end of the day, fairly substantial gains had been registered and the forward infantry elements had dug in solidly for the night. At 2200, however, enemy mortar and artillery fire suddenly increased on American positions and bursts of white phosphorous shells and colored smoke heralded the beginning of an anticipated counterattack. During the wild, two-and-a-half hour fracas fought at close quarters and often hand-to-hand, star shells and flares gave a weird cast to the battlefield. Gunfire support ships provided constant illumination over the scene of the fighting, and, with perfect timing, a reserve infantry company was committed into the line to help blunt the attack. The fight was over at midnight, and after daybreak the next day, unit identification of the nearly 500 Japanese dead revealed that fresh units – including some naval troops – had made the attack.

The main effort of the 6th Division attack on 21st May was mounted by the 4th Marines, with the 22nd Marines on the right pacing the attack while at the same time, providing fire support. Forward progress down the southern slopes of Sugar Loaf towards the easternmost limit of Horseshoe was slowed both by the bitter fighting all along the way as well as the treacherous footing underneath. Rain that fell during the morning and most of the afternoon turned the shell-torn slopes into slick mud-chutes, making all supply and evacuation almost impossible. But the fresh battalion in the attack overcame all obstacles to advance 200 yards.

Demolition and flamethrower teams blasted and burned the way in front of 3/4 as it drove into the extensive and well-prepared enemy positions in the interior of Horsehoe. By mid-afternoon, the deadly mortars emplaced there were destroyed and the Marines were solidly positioned in a defense line that extended approximately halfway between Horseshoe Hill and the Asato Gawa.

Intensive mortar and artillery fire from the Shuri heights combined with the rugged terrain in front of Half Moon restricted the use of armor and prevented the troops in that zone

Grenades were useful weapons against the tight Japanese defences

from advancing to any degree on the 21st. After five days of furious fighting and limited gains in the Half Moon area, Shepherd concluded that the bulk of enemy firepower preventing his division from making any gains in this sector was coming from the Shuri heights and outside of the division zone of action. He therefore decided to reorient the axis of his attack to the south and southwest rather than continuing to the southeast, where his troops had been receiving such destructive fire. He believed that this new maneuver would both relieve his forces of a threat to their left flank and at the same time give impetus to a drive to envelop Shuri from the west.

The enemy fire enfilading the 6th Division left flank was coming from positions directly in front of the 1st Division, which also was feeling the effects of Japanese weapons emplaced on commanding heights. At the time that Shepherd's Marines were first meeting opposition to their advance on Sugar Loaf, del Valle's division was clearing strongly held Dakeshi and entering Wana Draw, which, like other Japanese strongpoints in this area, held terrain that favored the defender.

As the 1st Division entered the forbidding Wana approaches to the Shuri hill mass, all evidence now signified that the main Japanese defenses in southern Okinawa consisted of a nearly regular series of concentric rings whose epicenter was protected by some of the most rugged terrain yet encountered in the drive south. The mission of breaching the Wana defenses fell to the 1st Marine and 77th Infantry Division at the same time that the 6th Marine and 96th Divisions attempted to envelop enemy flanks.

Analyzing the Wana positions after the battle, 1st Division Marines discovered that the Japanese had 'taken advantage of every feature of a terrain so difficult it could not have been better designed if the enemy himself had the power to do so.'

Preludes to the Shuri assault: heavy tank attacks (*above right*) and shelling (*below*) helped soften the defences

US M7 Priest Self-Propelled Howitzer
Based on the chassis of the earlier Medium M3 tanks, the Priest was an attempt
to allow a howitzer to keep up with rapidly advancing ground forces, and proved
to be very successful. *Weight:* **50,000 pounds.** *Armament:* **one 105mm howitzer
and a .5-inch Browning machine gun.** *Speed:* **26 mph on the road.** *Range:* **150
miles.** *Crew:* **seven.** *Engine:* **Ford V-8, 500 hp.** *Armour:* **$\frac{1}{2}$-inch plate at the front**

Utilizing every defense feature provided by nature, Ushijima had so
well organized the area that an assault
force attacking to the south would be
unable to bypass the main line of
resistance guarding Shuri, and would
instead have to penetrate directly
into the center of the heretofore un-
assailable defenses of the Thirty-
second Army.

The terrain within and immediately bordering the division zone was
both complex and varied. The
southernmost branch of the Asa
Kawa meandered along the gradually
rising floor of Wana Draw and through
the northerly part of Shuri. Low,
rolling ground on either side of the
stream offered neither cover nor
concealment against Japanese fire
coming from positions along the
reverse slope of Wana Ridge and the
military crest in the southern portion
of the zone. Approximately 400 yards

wide at its mouth, Wana Draw narrowed perceptibly as the stream
flowing through it approached the
town from which it derived its name.
Hill 55, a dominating piece of terrain
at the southern tip of the ridge,
guarded the western entry into the
draw. Bristling with nearly every
infantry weapon in the Japanese
arsenal, the positions on the hill had
clear fields of fire commanding all
approaches to the draw.

Before an all-out attack, del Valle
decided to neutralize the high ground
on both sides of Wana Draw. Tanks
and M-7s – the self-propelled 105mm
howitzers – were to shell the area
thoroughly before the assault battalion attempted to cross the open
ground at the mouth of the draw.
Tank-infantry teams worked over
the mouth of the draw during the
morning, and about mid-afternoon
they withdrew to clear the way for a

carrier-plane strike. Following this attack, the nine original tanks, reinforced by six others, continued the process of neutralizing the draw. At the end of the day, the commander of the 5th Marines commented that 'Wana Draw was another gorge like the one at Awacha . . . It was obvious that the position would have to be thoroughly pounded before it could be taken,' and then ordered the softening-up operations of the 15th continued the next day.

On 16th May, thirty tanks, four of them flamethrowers, supported the attack of 2/5 by burning and blasting enemy strongpoints in the Draw. Japanese antitank, artillery, and mortar fire was placed on the armored vehicles, disabling two and damaging two others. Before retiring at nightfall on this day, the 1st Tank Battalion had expended nearly 5,000 rounds of 75mm and 173,000 rounds of .30 caliber ammunition, and 600 gallons of napalm on targets on Dakeshi Ridge and Wana Draw that day. Following the two-day process of softening up provided by all supporting arms, the 5th Marines prepared to run the gauntlet of Wana Draw on the next day.

'Under the continued pounding of one of the most concentrated assaults in Pacific Warfare,' cracks appeared in the Shuri defenses on the 17th. Assault battalion troops worked over the caves and pillboxes lining the sides of the mouth to Wana Draw, and after undergoing terrifically heavy enemy fire, one infantry company finally succeeded in penetrating Japanese positions to establish a platoon-sized strongpoint on Hill 55. Despite intermittent mortar and artillery shelling during the night of 17th-18th May, the position held, while Wana Ridge was attacked by 3/7, to the right of the 5th Marines. An abbreviated analysis by the division fairly well summarized that day's fighting: 'Gains were measured by yards won, lost, then won again.'

Pinned down by heavy enemy fire from the reverse slope of Hill 55, the isolated platoon could neither advance nor withdraw, so it remained where it was, supplied by tanks which brought ammunition and rations forward. The 1st Division's bitter contest for possession of Wana Draw continued on 19th May along the same bloody lines experienced the previous four days. The 7th Marines made the major effort for the division, while the 5th Marines continued to punish and be punished at the mouth of Wana Draw.

Despite the devastation being visited upon them by the 5th Marines and its supporting tanks, the Japanese built new positions in Wana Draw daily, and reconstructed and again camouflaged by night old ones that Marine tank fire had exposed and damaged by day. As the assault infantry plunged further into the draw, and as the draw itself narrowed, an increasing number of Japanese defensive positions conspired with the rugged terrain to make passage more difficult. Dominating the eastern end of Wana Ridge on the northwestern outskirts of Shuri was 110 Meter Hill, which commanded a view of the zones of both the 1st Marine and 77th Infantry Divisions. Defensive fire from this position stymied the final reduction of Japanese holdings in Wana Draw and eventual capture of the Shuri redoubt.

Tanks, M-7s, 37mm guns, and overhead machine gun fire supported the 19th May attacks against Wana Ridge and 110 Meter Hill, and by mid-afternoon assault troops managed to secure a goodly portion of the ridge with the exception of the summit of the hill. The next day, tanks burned and blasted their way forward to destroy enemy-held caves and fortified positions blocking the offense, while the attacking Marines moved within hand grenade-throwing range of Wana Ridge defenders. When the northern slope of the ridge had been gained, the assault troops found they could not budge the Japanese soldiers in reverse-slope positions. An attempt was made to burn them out by rolling barrels of napalm down the hill into Japanese emplacements in Wana Draw and then igniting them by exploding white phosphorous grenades on top of the containers. Unfortunately, the terrain prevented the barrels from rolling all the way down into the draw, and in the end, the enemy sustained little damage and few injuries from this hasty field expedient. The Marines dug in for the night on top of the ridge, and their positions here led to considerable mortar, hand grenade, and sniper fire, as well as the usually lively and abusive exchange of curses and threats of bodily harm that often took place when the combatants were within shouting distance of each other. One Marine officer, an old 'China hand,' who spoke fluent Japanese, amused himself by thoroughly cursing out the enemy and richly insulting them in their own language with every appropriate word he had in his extensive vocabulary.

On the right of the 1st Division zone, troops of the 5th Marines attacked on the 20th to gain their objective, an area running roughly from Hill 55 southwest to the Naha-Shuri road. A continuous artillery barrage was laid on Shuri Ridge, the western extension of the commanding height on which Shuri Castle had been built, as assault units quickly worked their way towards the objective and secured it by noon. Capture of Hill 55 would mean that the 1st Division would hold positions providing more favorable jumping-off points for a concerted effort against Ushijima's headquarters.

At dawn on 21st May, 2/1 – on the corps boundary – moved out against heavy opposition to secure the summit of 110 Meter Hill and the rest of Wana Ridge. The supporting armor, which had been so effective to this time, was limited by the irregular and steep nature of the terrain and could provide the assault elements with overhead fire only. A deep cleft at the head of the draw prevented the Shermans from getting behind the enemy and taking reverse slope positions under fire. It was also learned that, as the draw approached the village of Wana, its walls rose to sheer heights ranging from 200 to 300 feet, and lining the wall faces were numerous, well-defended caves ·that were unapproachable to all but the suicidally inclined. No assault straight up the draw was to be successful unless preceded by an intense preparation by all supporting arms, less the armor which could not operate in the steep terrain forward of Wana. Darkening skies and constant rain

squalls obscured the battlefield to enemy and friendly observers alike as the Marines attempted to clear out reverse slope positions on Wana Ridge in a coordinated tank-infantry effort. According to the plan, the assault company and the tanks would attack up Wana Draw, while, supporting the attack from the crest of the ridge, the remainder of the infantry battalion committed in this attack would be prepared to drive straight across the ridge in order to gain the objectives – Hill 55 and the ridgeline to the east. By 1800, Hill 55 was in friendly hands, but the Marines were unable to push further east towards Shuri.

The miserable weather prevailing all day on 21st May worsened at midnight when the drizzle became a deluge, seriously limiting all |visibility. As these conditions favored a counterattack, the Japanese took advantage of the situation, and 200 enemy troops scrambled up Wana Ridge to strike at the Marines in night defensive positions there. A few positions were overrun, but were recaptured the following day as the Americans restored their lines.

Torrential rains beginning the night of 21st-22nd May continued for the rest of the month and on into June. This continuous downpour almost halted the tortuous 1st Division drive towards Shuri. Terrain factors and a determined enemy stand in the Wana area seriously restricted tank activity in the 5th Marines zone, which held the only ground favoring armored tactics. Under these conditions, which conspired to reinforce the Japanese defenses, the 1st Division was faced with the alternatives of moving ahead against all odds or continuing the existing stalemate. To make either choice was difficult, for both presented a bloody prospect.

For Geiger's IIIAC, the period of 15th-21st May was marked by the struggles of his divisions to capture two key Japanese strongpoints – Sugar Loaf Hill and Wana Draw. During these same seven days, XXIV Corps units fought a series of difficult battles to gain the strongly defended hills and ridges blocking the approaches to Yonabaru and Shuri. These barriers, curiously named

Above: Camouflaged howitzer emplacement. *Below:* Correspondents interview Generals Clement and Shepherd during a lull in the fighting

Chocolate Drop, Flat Top, Hogback, Love, Dick, Oboe, and Sugar gained fleeting fame when they became the scenes of bitter and prolonged contests. But, when XXIV Corps had turned the eastern flank of Shuri defenses and anticipated imminent success, the Army attack – like that of the Marines – became bogged down and was brought to a standstill in the heavy rainfall and muddy terrain.

On 15th May, the 77th Division continued its grinding advance in the middle of the Tenth Army line against the hard core of the Thirty-second Army defenses at Shuri. In coordination with its own assault against Dick Hill, the 96th Division supported the 77th's attack against Flat Top Hill. Those Army troops already on Conical Hill found forward movement difficult, and dangerous as well, because of overwhelming fire coming from another hill complex southwest of their positions. In addition, the enemy's 89th Regiment held formidable and well-organized defenses on the reverse slopes of Conical, and prevented any advance to the south. Although murderous enemy crossfire on the next day again stopped the infantry from making any significant gains, a platoon of 96th Division tanks ran the gauntlet of fire sweeping the coastal flat and advanced 1,000 yards to enter the northwestern outskirts of Yonabaru. Here, the Shermans lashed the ruins of the town, and the enemy suspected of being therein, with 75mm and machine gun fire. Heavy Japanese fire in turn, covering the southern slopes of Conical, prevented the infantry from exploiting the rapid armor penetration, however. After exhausting their ammunition supply, the tanks withdrew to the line of departure.

On the right flank of the 96th Division line, American troops attempted to expand their hold on Dick Hill and, after a violent bayonet and hand grenade fight at close quarters, managed to gain only a few yards before machine gun fire from Oboe Hill forced a halt. To the right of the 96th Division, 77th Infantry Division troops were experiencing the same extremely accurate and vicious machine gun fire and mortar barrages as they attempted an attack on Flat Top and Chocolate Drop Hills.

A very successful predawn attack by the 77th Division on the 17th surprised the Japanese and forced them to give way. The Army troops made some very substantial gains and garnered commanding terrain, including Chocolate Drop Hill. At the end of the day, the 77th's infantry battalions were only a few hundred yards away from Shuri and Ishimmi. Troops following the assault elements spent the day in mopping up, sealing cave positions and burial vaults, and neutralizing those enemy strongpoints bypassed in the early-morning surprise maneuver.

Although remnants of the Japanese 22nd Regiment were still holding the reverse slopes of Flat Top and Dick Hills, for all practical purposes, the regiment existed in name only, for it had been practically wiped out in the attack on Chocolate Drop on 17th May. American attacks across the entire defense line fronting Shuri had just about depleted many of the experienced units Ushijima had available, although the enemy was fully able to take advantage of the natural, fortress-like properties of the region he was defending, and could, in some places, defend in depth to contain potential American penetrations. Should the Tenth Army forces break through, though, Ushijima had few reserves remaining to call upon.

Both XXIV Corps front line divisions pushed forward slowly but steadily the next two days to get ever closer to the heart of the Shuri defenses. On 19th May, the 77th Division systematically began to eliminate Japanese firing positions in 110 Meter Hill, Ishimmi Ridge, and the reverse slopes of Flat Top and Dick Hills. All of these positions had provided the enemy with good observation and clear fields of fire which commanded terrain over which the Americans were advancing. Every weapon in the 77th's arsenal capable of doing so placed destructive fire on the enemy emplacements. While these missions were being fired, the infantry fought off a series of counterattacks growing in size and fury as darkness fell. The Japanese were finally turned back at dawn on the 20th when all available artillery was called down on them.

Hard, grinding fighting all across the Tenth Army line fronting Shuri inexorably led to a compression of Japanese defenses and finally resulted in 77th Division troops entering the outskirts of Shuri itself. During this period of the battle, however, every American yard was gained only because of the individual soldier's sheer guts and efforts in the face of an unbelievably fanatic enemy determination to hold against all odds. To strengthen the attack on Shuri, which he saw could be outflanked as he watched the progress of the 96th Division down the east coast, on 20th May Hodges alerted the 7th Infantry Division to its imminent commitment in the fighting and ordered it to move to assembly areas north of Conical Hill. Two days later, the division entered the line and attacked to take the high ground north of Yonabaru.

The rain which began on 21st May continued and intensified to become soaking torrents before the assault elements of the 7th Division were even in jump-off positions. In no time at all, 'the road to Yonabaru from the north – the only supply road from established bases in the 7th Division zone – became impassable to wheeled vehicles and within two or three days disappeared and had to be abandoned.' Like the Tenth Army divisions on the west coast, those on the east were effectively held up by the mud and the rain, which now seemed to be allied with Ushijima and his Thirty-second Army.

Disregarding the weather and sloppy terrain, the 7th Division successfully pushed through the enemy manning the Ozato Hills, a rugged and complex terrain mass paralleling Nakagusuku Wan and lying between Yonabaru and the Chinen Peninsula, IIIAC units pushed forward on the west coast on 22nd May. Forward elements of the 6th Division crossed the shallow portion of the Asato Gawa and moved into the outskirts of Naha before drawing any fire. Although the flanking divisions of the Tenth Army were making encouraging progress, the 1st Marine and 77th and 96th Infantry Divisions in the center of the line found success to be an elusive thing during the week of 22nd May. Added to a fanatic Japanese defense was the rain and the resultant sea of mud, which forced the troops to wallow rather than maneuver. Under these conditions, infantry units could only probe and patrol ahead of their respective zones.

The rain continued for nine days, and ranged from light scattered showers to drowning deluges. In the end, the entire southern front became a vast morass that bogged down both men and machines. Because TAF planes had been grounded and could not fly supply drops, all supplies had to be manhandled to the front. Tired, worn out foot troops from both front line and reserve units were pressed into action and formed into carrying parties.

Under these conditions, the engineers worked round the clock relentlessly to keep the road net between forward supply dumps and the front lines in operating condition. But continued use by trucks and tracked vehicles caused the roads to be closed, but only after the mud itself had bemired and stalled the vehicles. As a result, division commanders found it next to impossible to build up and maintain reserve stocks of the supplies needed to support a full-scale assault. With the movement of Tenth Army forces all but stopped, the entire front became stalemated. To alleviate the situation, landing and unloading sites were developed on both coasts, and LSTs as well as other landing vessels and vehicles were employed to bring supplies down the coasts from the main beaches and dumps in the north.

In assessing the American threat to Shuri by the American advances down both coasts, Ushijima, his commanders, and his staff believed that the Thirty-second Army was 'still able to halt the collapse of all positions by holding positions in depth to the line of Shichina and Kokuba' even though the Marines had 'broken into the city of Naha.' This evaluation was tempered somewhat by the realization that Thirty-second Army troops would 'be unable to maintain their Shuri front' if the American

With the powerful support of a tank, 6th Division Marines thrust through the outskirts into Naha

spearhead in the Naha-Yonabaru valley was not blunted. To stem the tide of the XXIV Corps attack against his positions north and east of Shuri, Ushijima threw every available man into a defense line that began on the southwest slopes of Conical Hill, ran through Yonawa, and was anchored at the road junction in the village of Chan.

By 25th May, the 7th Infantry Division, which had forced the enemy from commanding terrain features in front of it, inserted an opening wedge into the southeastern defenses of Shuri. On the opposite coast, the 6th Division's troops entered and occupied the once-urban, now-razed area of Naha west of a canal which ran through the city. Across most of the rest of the Tenth Army line, however, high water and mud still limited infantry operations to patrolling only. Troops holding positions in the 96th Division zone south and west of Conical Hill were all but isolated from rear area facilities and suffered serious

losses under a rash of small counterattacks and continual enemy infiltration attempts. The depleted infantry companies holding the line were thus forced to utilize all available manpower from battalion and regimental headquarters units. The front line organizations put these men into the line or assigned them the tremendous wearying task of handcarrying supplies forward over the glutinous terrain. Descriptive of these agonized efforts is a comment made by an officer of the 96th Division, who said: 'Those on the forward slopes slid down. Those on the reverse slopes slid back. Otherwise, no change.'

Possibly a favorable portent for the future and a happy change in the otherwise gloomy reports coming in from the bogged-down units occurred on 26th May, when it appeared as though the enemy was pulling out of Shuri. Observers at the 1st and 5th Marines observation posts reported that there was a good deal of enemy movement south, and the 1st Division G-2 then requested an aerial surveillance of the suspected area at noon.

Despite hazardous flying conditions in the rain and poor visibility, which in themselves would severely limit the value and amount of information that could be gained, a spotter plane was catapulted almost immediately from one of the capital ships in the anchorage after receipt of the 1st Division request. Upon his arrival over the target area, the aerial observer confirmed the presence of a large number of Japanese troops and vehicles clogging the roads leading south from Shuri.

Within thirteen minutes after this sighting, the cruiser *New Orleans* had fired the first salvo in a continued and devastating barrage brought to bear on the withdrawing enemy by artillery, mortars, the main and secondary batteries of gunfire support ships, and the machine guns and bombs of Marine aircraft that had risen from sodden fields to harry the Japanese from above. Ushijima's hopes for a undiscovered withdrawal under the inclement weather conditions were shattered by the massed fires which caught and blasted some 3-4,000 of his troops with their tanks, vehicles, and artillery pieces in the open. The pilots of small observation planes zoomed through the overcast to treetop height, and lower, to count and report back an estimated 500 enemy killed. Commending the fliers for their day's work, del Valle sent a message reading, 'Congratulations and thanks for prompt response this afternoon when the Nips where caught on road with kimonos down.'

Continuing stubborn reluctance on the part of some Japanese to give way to the American attack seemed to belie the fact that Ushijima's forces were indeed withdrawing. Nonetheless, artillery batteries and naval gun-fire ships fired continuous harassing and interdiction missions on all routes, road junctions, and crossroads in the area leading south from Shuri. To keep the enemy off balance and unable to make a stand, and to exploit the implications inherent in the Japanese withdrawal, on 27th May Buckner ordered his corps commanders to initiate strong and unrelenting pressure on the enemy to determine his intentions and to keep the opposition otherwise disorganized. Furthermore, the Tenth Army commander strongly emphasized the fact that Ushijima's troops must not be permitted to establish new, secure positions with only minimal interference.

A full-scale attack all across the front was precluded however, by the continuous rains and their effect on the terrain. The Tenth Army therefore settled for aggressive patrol action against Japanese strongpoints still holding out against American incursions. Apparently contradicting the observed enemy withdrawal and the effect it should have had on easing the Iceberg situation, patrol reports reaching front line division command posts read, 'Does not appear that resistance has lessened,' or, 'No indication of Japanese withdrawal,' and implied that Shuri would not yet, if ever, fall easily.

On the east coast, 7th Division units reached Inasomi, approximately two miles southwest of Yonabaru, without meeting any organized resistance on 27th May, and in the 6th Division zone on the opposite coast, the remainder of Naha was taken. The beginning of the end for Shuri came on 28th May, according to 1st Division accounts, when both the Marines and 77th Division troops took high ground to the north and east of the city. Tuesday 29th May 1945, is the significant date in the history of the Okinawa campaign, for it was on this day that elements of the 1st Marine Division captured Shuri Castle, once the seat of the rulers of Okinawa.

The 5th Marines attacked at 0730 on the 29th, with its 1st Battalion on the left and the 3rd Battalion on the right. The fire of enemy machine guns, mortars and small arms paced the advance of the assault troops, but was unable to halt the momentum of their attack. Lieutenant-Colonel Charles W Shelburne's 1/5 moved rapidly over muddy terrain against little opposition and immediately occupied Shuri's ridge crest in close proximity to the castle. From this position, at approximately 0930, the battalion commander requested permission from del Valle to send an assault company to storm the fortification, which seemed to be lightly manned. Despite the fact that the castle itself was within the zone

of the 77th Infantry Division, del Valle granted the request. He believed that the capture of this important enemy strongpoint would favorably effect and shorten the campaign; this opportunity, therefore, had to be seized at once. Shortly after the island was secured, the 1st Division commander offered the opinion that, 'at that time the position of the 77th Division was such that it would have taken several hard days' fighting through enemy resistance' if he had waited for the tactical situation to unfold normally.

Bowling over the few Japanese that were in their way, Marines from Company A, 1/5, under Captain Julian D Dusenbury, drove east along the ridge and right into the castle itself, securing it at 1015. The company commander, a native of South Carolina, created somewhat of a stir in the Tenth Army, when he raised the Confederate Stars and Bars, rather than the national colors, over the castle.

The 77th Division had programmed an air strike and a heavy artillery bombardment on the bastion for 29th May and had received warning of the Marine attack only a few short minutes before it was mounted. Bruce and his staff worked frantically to contact all supporting arms agencies and were just 'barely able to avert called strikes in time.' He had been given no indication by the 1st Division that it intended entering the 77th's zone, nor had permission to do so been requested, as is usually customary under such circumstances. 'Had timely notice been given and the move been properly coordinated,' Bruce believed that '77 Div could have rendered adequate support to the Marines . . .' Overshadowing this near tragedy was the fact that the Marine success resulted from the close teamwork of the Tenth Army support and assault troops who had not permitted the enemy to relax for an instant. Without this unrelenting pressure, the breakthrough would not have been possible.

Once his troops were inside the castle, the 3/5 commander set up the remainder of his battalion in perimeter defense around its battered walls. At no time after the capture of

The razed city of Naha

Shuri Castle was there any indication that the Japanese defenders of the hills north of the city and in such key areas as Wana Draw were either being worn down or concerned with the presence of American units in their rear. Reports from Tenth Army forces all along the line gave proof that enemy resistance remained undiminished in its stubbornness. Only in a goodly portion of Chinen Peninsula, scouted by 7th Division troops during the day, was there little or no opposition.

Offsetting the relatively uninhibited advance down the coasts by Tenth Army flanking divisions, a vividly contrasted picture was presented by the massive struggle through the center of the island. Despite the efforts of Buckner's forces to execute a mass double envelopment successfully and to encircle the bulk of Ushijima's troops at Shuri, all signs pointed up the fact that the Japanese rear guard had accomplished its mission well – the majority of the units defending Shuri had indeed escaped to the south.

Breakout
to the
south

Ushijima's decision to abandon his Shuri defenses was made at a conference at the Thirty-second Army command post on the night of 22nd May, when the Japanese commander was forced to re-evaluate the battle plans he had adopted in March. The only item on the agenda of this momentous staff meeting was a discussion of how best to prevent – or at least forestall – the disaster threatening to engulf the Thirty-second Army. According to original contingency plans calling for a massive defense centering about Shuri, in face of imminent defeat all Japanese units located elsewhere on Okinawa and still able to fight would withdraw on order for a last-ditch stand in the vicinity of the army command post.

Tactical conditions at the time of the May conference, however, precluded activation of this plan, for, if Shuri was to be held to the end, approximately 50,000 Japanese troops would have to be compressed into a final defense sector less than a mile in diameter. Not only would these close quarters prevent the establish-

ment of an effective defense, the soldiers here would be lined up like ducks in a shooting gallery and easy targets for overwhelming American fire.

In discussing the alternatives to remaining at Shuri, Ushijima's commanders and staff considered two other areas – Chinen Peninsula, which had been organized for a defense before L-Day, and the Kiyamu Peninsula, at the southern tip of Okinawa. In face of obvious evidence against Chinen, Kiyamu was selected as the best area in which the Thirty-second Army could develop a solid defense for prolonging the battle. Dominated by the Yaeju Dake-Yuza Dake Escarpment, this area contained a number of natural and man-made caves in which the Japanese could store supplies and at the same time protect their troops against the Tenth Army bombardments. The terrain on the peninsula had been organized for a defense earlier by the 24th Division, which had also cached a large store of weapons and ammunition there before it was ordered north into the Shuri defense line. As opposed to the poor road net into Chinen, all roads south led directly to the proposed new positions and would permit the army to make a rapid mass movement out of the Shuri lines. On the other hand, Tenth Army tanks could also move south over these roads, but only to the outpost defenses of the sector, for the sheer cliffs, steep hills, and deep ridges of the area would deny further passage to armored vehicles. In this broken terrain, the infantry would be on its own.

Not all of the senior Japanese leaders approved of the planned withdrawal. One dissenter was Lieutenant-General Takeo Fujioka, commander of the 62nd Division. His objection was based on a compassion for the thousands of severely wounded men who could not be taken south. He felt most strongly about this point because it had been his division that was originally assigned to defend Shuri, and his officers and men had taken the brunt of American attacks on the city. He contended, therefore, that their desire to fight to the last in their present positions should be

fulfilled. Unmoved by this plea, Ushijima ordered the division south.

According to the revised defense plan, the 44th Independent Mixed Brigade would move from its positions on the westernmost flank of the Shuri front to take up defense positions on a line running from Hanagusuku on the east coast to Yaeju Dake. Assigned to occupy the commanding heights of the Yaeju Dake-Yuza Dake Escarpment, the ridges of Mezado and Kunishi, and Nagusuku on the west coast was the 24th Division. Elements of both of these two organizations would also establish and defend an outpost line – and the zone forward of it – running from Itoman through Yunagusuku and Gushichan. The heavily depleted forces of the 62nd Division would occupy positions along the southern coast in the rear of the main battle line. In these positions, Fujioka's units could reorganize and, at the same time, be prepared to reinforce threatened positions at the front, on order. The firing batteries of Major Wada's 5th Artillery Command were ordered emplaced within a triangularly shaped area formed by Kunishi, Makabe, and Medeera, and assigned a mission in direct support of the front. The Thirty-second Army reserve was made up of the Okinawa Naval Base Force, which was to remain on Oroku Peninsula and then move, on order, to an assembly area in the center of Kiyamu. Finally, as each unit on the Shuri line broke contact with the Americans, it was to leave a sufficiently strong force in position to keep Tenth Army attackers occupied long enough to guarantee a successful withdrawal.

In order that Ushijima could organize his new dispositions in the south, the force remaining on the Shuri front was to hold until 31st May. Behind this line, withdrawing units would leave other rear guard elements strong enough to maintain a stiff defense line running along the Kokuba River to the hills north of Tsukasan and Chan until the night of 2nd June. At that time, the line would then cut south through Karadera to the east coast. Approximately 2,000 yards further south, another temporary line – this one centered on Tomusu – would be established and held until the night of 4th June. Thirty-second Army staff planners believed that the time gained during holding actions along these lines would permit the organization and manning of the final outpost zone. Before beginning its own retreat south, the composite naval unit on Oroku Peninsula was to guard the western flank of the withdrawal route.

All available replacements were thrown into the disintegrating Shuri front on 23rd May when the onsurging Tenth Army forced Ushijima to bolster his defenses. The first Japanese transportation to head south departed Shuri at midnight of 23rd-24th May, carrying wounded and a portion of the army ammunition supply. On the 24th, the first walking wounded began leaving caves that passed as hospitals. Many terminal cases, too seriously wounded to be moved, were either given a lethal injection of morphine, or – less mercifully – left behind to suffer a lingering end without benefit of the relief-giving drug. Limited medical care of the wounded appears to have been commonplace and forced more by circumstances than wilful neglect.

Following the withdrawal plan, the main body of the Shuri force was to begin the southerly trek on 29th May, and with the arrival of dawn on the 30th, the greater portion of the Thirty-second Army had successfully postponed its final reckoning at the hands of the Tenth Army by pulling out of Shuri and out of the grasp of Buckner's flanking division. Taking advantage of the heavy rains and the accompanying poor visibility, Ushijima had executed a 'properly deft' withdrawal to establish his new army headquarters outside of Mabuni, eleven miles south of Shuri, in a cave deep within Hill 89. By this time, his covering forces were in position to slow down a Tenth Army pursuit and thereby gave the Thirty-second Army a bit more time to organize the defense of Kiyamu Peninsula.

American attempts to exploit the successful breakthrough at Shuri and to maintain incessant pressure on the reeling Thirty-second Army were frustrated on the 30th by an electrical storm accompanied by torrential

rains on an already oversaturated landscape. Movement of all Tenth Army units was effectively halted by the mud. Amphibious craft and vehicles were employed on both coasts to provide logistical support to the two corps and to enable the ground commanders to maintain at least minimum supply levels.

Out of a total of 916 missions of all sorts flown by Marine Torpedo Bomber Squadron 232 in May, seventy-four were air drops of supplies to support front line troops and advance patrols. The weather situation changed so abruptly at the end of the month, that for the first time no enemy planes were detected in the area for the twenty-four-hour period ending at midnight on the 30th. The heavy rain, however, did not completely halt ground activity that day, for attacks were made all long the Tenth Army front. While attempting to locate the headquarters of the Thirty-second Army at Shuri Castle on the 30th, intelligence representatives from the 1st Marine Division discovered numerous caves containing many enemy documents of intelligence value. Together with these

Tropical storms turn Okinawa into a mudfield reminiscent of World War 1 and halt the Marines' advance

G-2 section personnel, del Valle sent the division colors to the battalion commander of 3/1 with a request that they be raised over the castle. After locating the remnants of a Japanese flagpole, the Marines erected it near the southern wall of the battered battlement, raised the flag, and then the 3/1 CO ordered everybody in the area to 'haul ass' because he anticipated that the Japanese would use the flagpole as an aiming point and would fire an artillery concentration on the excellent target almost immediately.

The steady advances of the Tenth Army flank divisions was slowed on 31st May, when the 6th Marine and 7th Infantry Divisions met firmer resistance as they renewed their attacks. It appeared that the Iceberg force had overcome the seemingly impregnable Shuri redoubt only to run into the newly organized defenses positioned along the Kokuba River on the west coast and north of Tsuka-san. Since the time of the initial

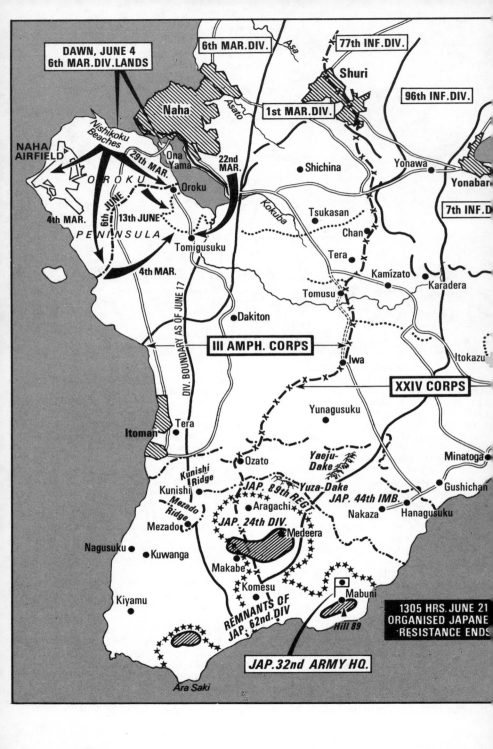

DAWN, JUNE 4
6th MAR. DIV. LANDS

6th MAR. DIV.

77th INF. DIV.

Shuri

96th INF. DIV.

1st MAR. DIV.

Naha

Nishikoku Beaches

NAHA AIRFIELD

Ona Yama

29th MAR.

22nd MAR.

Shichina

Yonawa

Yonabar

OROKU

Oroku

6th JUNE

4th MAR.

13th JUNE

P E N I N S U L A

4th MAR.

Kokuba

Tsukasan

7th INF. D

Tomigusuku

Asato

Chan

Tera

Kamizato

Karadera

Tomusu

Dakiton

DIV. BOUNDARY AS OF JUNE 17

III AMPH. CORPS

Iwa

Itokazu

XXIV CORPS

Yunagusuku

Tera

Itoman

Ozato

Yaeju-Dake

Minatoga

Kunishi Ridge

Kunishi

Yuza-Dake

Gushichan

JAP. 89th REGT.

JAP. 44th IMB.

Mezado Ridge

Aragachi

Nakaza

Hanagusuku

Mezado

JAP. 24th DIV.

Medeera

Nagusuku

Kuwanga

Makabe

Komesu

Mabuni

Kiyama

REMNANTS OF JAP. 62nd DIV.

Hill 89

1305 HRS. JUNE 21 ORGANISED JAPANE ·RESISTANCE ENDS

JAP. 32nd ARMY HQ.

Ara Saki

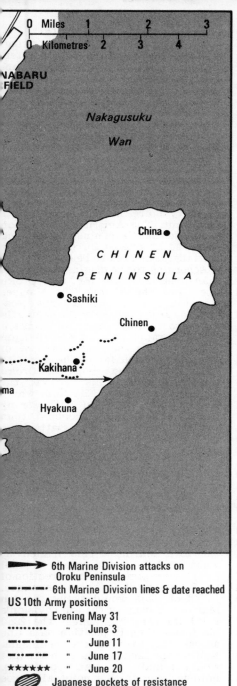

Miles / Kilometres scale

NABARU FIELD

Nakagusuku Wan

China ●

CHINEN PENINSULA

● Sashiki

Chinen ●

Kakihana

Hyakuna ●

6th Marine Division attacks on Oroku Peninsula

━━━ 6th Marine Division lines & date reached

US 10th Army positions

━━ ━━ Evening May 31
••••••••• " June 3
━•━•━•• " June 11
━••━••━••• " June 17
★★★★★★ " June 20

Japanese pockets of resistance

landings on L-Day, Buckner's forces had killed an estimated 62,548 enemy troops while capturing only 465 others in sixty-one days of bloody endeavor. The Tenth Army had seized all but eight square miles of Okinawa, and that parcel of land was becoming a pocket of doom into which the remnants of Ushijima's army were being driven. The battle so far had cost the Americans 5,309 dead, 23,909 wounded, and 346 missing in action.

While the remainder of the Tenth Army continued its push to the south, on 1st June Shepherd and his 6th Marine Division had been given thirty-six hours to prepare for an amphibious assault on Oroku Peninsula. To replace 6th Division units in the IIIAC line, the division boundary was changed and del Valle's division assumed responsibility for Shepherd's former zone. Reconnaissance scouts from the 6th Division reconnoitered the peninsula during the hours of darkness on 1st-2nd June and reported that Oroku was still occupied by Japanese troops, but not in strength.

By noon of the 2nd, Shepherd had received final instructions for the landing, for which his staff had already begun detailed planning. After examining all possible courses of action, he decided to land over the Nishikoku beaches on the northeast corner of the peninsula. Owing to a shortage of amphibious tractors then prevailing on Okinawa, only seventy-two could be made available for the landing. Most of the other LVTs were in poor condition as a result of extensive and constant employment during the period of heavy rains and washed-out roads. Nevertheless, with the amtracs he had been allotted, Shepherd planned to land his division in a column of regiments with the 4th Marines in the assault.

The 6th Division forces mounted out from assembly areas near the mouths of the Asato and Asa Rivers, while supplies and tanks were loaded at a point that had been developed near Machinato airfield. Because it would be difficult to maintain a waterborne resupply operation during the fighting

Okinawa south of Naha: the final three weeks

on the peninsula, the 6th Division commander decided to capture Ono Yama, a small island in Naha harbor which connected the city with Oroku, at the same time his troops landed on the peninsula. After its capture by 6th Reconnaissance Company Marines reinforced by an armored amtrac unit, the island served the division as a logistic support base located fairly close to the fighting.

K-Day, the day of the landing, was set for 4th June. The reinforced division scout company was to land on Ono Yama at 0500 and the main assault force on Oroku forty-five minutes later. In the early morning darkness of K-Day, troops and equipment were loaded aboard the LVTs according to plan. An intense pre-landing bombardment lasting an hour was laid down on the target. During their approach to the line of departure, the assault troops were treated to the spectacle of the furious lashing given the beach area as over 4,300 high explosive shells ranging in caliber from 75mm to 14-inch blasted suspected enemy positions on the high ground immediately behind the beaches. Participating in this cannonading were the guns of one battleship, two heavy cruisers, one destroyer, and fifteen battalions of artillery.

Intelligence estimates of enemy strength had indicated that the peninsula was defended by 1,200-1,500 Japanese troops. At 0600, the first Marines landed against no opposition on the beach and were able to rush inland for about 300 yards to the high ground under only desultory machine gun fire. Once ashore, the assault forces found the terrain very open and generally flat, but as they moved inland to the central, southern, and western portions of the peninsula, the Marines encountered many ridges and steep hills. The hills initially captured were unoccupied but close inspection revealed that the terrain was honeycombed with connecting tunnels and numerous firing ports, which, when manned, had given the defenders a commanding, all-around view of the area.

At the end of the first day ashore on Oroku, against steadily increasing resistance, the 6th Division gained

1,500 yards. For the next ten days, Shepherd's troops fought a slogging, difficult campaign against a determined enemy, which, like the Japanese encountered in front of Shuri, used the terrain to advantage. Because of the complex, cross-compartmented nature of the ground, compounded by the heavy overgrowth of tangled vegetation, it appeared as though the 6th Division was fighting the battle for Motobu Peninsula all over again. Although many of the Japanese on Oroku Peninsula had been killed after three days of fighting, the stubborn opposition of those still alive caused casualty figures in the rifle regiments to mount. The Americans also soon surmised that the peninsula was being defended by greater forces than were initially estimated to be there.

According to the original scheme of maneuver adopted for the Oroku operation, the 4th and 29th Marines would drive in a southeasterly direction towards the base of the peninsula and into the main part of Okinawa. But the rapid pace of the division attack during the first four days of the operation had forced the enemy to withdraw to the south of Oroku village and, with his back to the Kokuba River, into the hills which were heavily invested with strong defensive positions. Shepherd then reoriented the axis of his attack to the northeast, formally recognizing the course the battle was taking.

By this time, the 4th Marines on the right of the division line had advanced much further than the stalled 29th Marines in the division zone on the left. When the new attack order was issued, the 4th was in the process of pivoting in a counterclockwise movement on the right flank elements of the 29th Marines. This maneuver, when ended, would head Colonel Shapley's regiment in the direction of the hard core of Japanese resistance. In effect, this would swing the 4th Marines in front of the 6th Division's third infantry regiment – the 22nd Marines – then in position on a line across the base of the peninsula. Neither the 22nd nor the 29th Marines would remain in static positions, however, for at this point all three regiments were moving and inexorably tightening the circle around the hapless Okinawa Naval Base Force.

In the course of the fighting on the 9th, the attacking Marines found little that was different from the previous days of fighting on the peninsula, for 'the advance was still slow and tedious against bitter resistance. Every Jap seemed to be armed with a machine gun, and there was still some light and heavy mortar fire. Casualties continue to mount and the number of Japs killed soared over the maximum of 1500 which were supposed to have been defending, and there were still plenty left.'

As the three 6th Division regiments converged on the Oroku garrison from different directions, and completely isolated it from the main body of the Thirty-second Army at Kiyamu, Ota's mixed defense force was slowly compressed into a small pocket in the southeast region of the peninsula. On all levels, infantry commanders found it increasingly difficult to maintain unit control and to coordinate the employment of their supporting fires with those of adjacent units because of the limitations imposed by restricted zones of action. These conditions, together with the stubborn terrain and the no-less yielding defense, tended to slow to some degree all of the attacking Marine battalions.

Aware that the end of his Oroku garrison force was not too far distant, on 6th June Ota sent the following message to his superiors in Tokyo:

'More than two months have passed since we engaged the invaders. In complete unity and harmony with the Army, we have made every effort to crush the enemy.

Despite our efforts the battle is going against us. My own troops are at a disadvantage since all available heavy guns and four crack battalions of naval landing forces were allocated to Army command. Also, enemy equipment is superior to our own.

I herewith tender my deepest apology to the Emperor for my failure to better defend the Empire, the grave task with which I was entrusted.

The troops under my command have fought gallantly, in the finest tradition of the Japanese Navy. Fierce bombing and bombardments may deform the mountains of Okinawa, but cannot alter the loyal spirit of our men. We hope and pray for the perpetuation of the Empire and gladly give our lives for that goal.

To the Navy Minister and all my superior officers I tender sincerest appreciation and gratitude for their kindness of many years. At the same time, I earnestly beg you to give thoughtful consideration to the families of my men who fall at this outpost as soldiers of the Emperor.

With my officers and men I give three cheers for the Emperor and pray for the everlasting peace of the Empire.

Though my body decay in remote Okinawa,

My spirit will persist in defense of the homeland.

Minoru Ota

Naval Commander'

Four days after the transmission of the above, Ota released his last dispatch to his immediate commander, Ushijima, reading, 'Enemy groups are now attacking our cave headquarters. The Naval Base Force is dying gloriously at this moment . . . We are grateful for your past kindnesses and pray for the success of the Army.'

By late afternoon of 12th June, the last Japanese strongpoint in the zone of the 29th Marines was taken. Having lost this key terrain feature, enemy troops were forced to flee to the alluvial flatlands along the Kokuba River coast. Here, they 'began displaying flags of surrender. Language officers equipped with loudspeaker systems were dispatched to the front line areas to assist in the surrender of those Japanese who desired to (do so). The attempt was partially successful, eight-six enemy soldiers voluntarily laid down their arms.'

The 6th Division made a final sweep of the remaining Japanese-held area with two infantry battalions in the attack on 13th June. Advancing rapidly to the southeast, they were joined by a third battalion. Approaching the river flats, the attackers formed into skirmish lines, and flushed the Japanese from the marshy grasslands along the river bank. A number of enemy soldiers gave themselves up, some committed suicide, others fought to the bitter end, and a few stoically awaited their deaths. Two observers viewing the fighting from the north shore of the Naha estuary, at a point about 1,000 yards across the water from Oroku, 'saw the Marines come up over the high ground from the south and close in on the Japanese . . . The last survivor was a Japanese officer who calmly walked over to the seawall, sat down, lit a cigarette, and waited for the Marines to kill him.'

Marine assault troops reached the seawall on the river bank at noon and spent the rest of the day ferreting out small enemy groups attempting to evade death or capture by hiding in the cane fields and rice paddies near the river. At 1750 on 13th June, Shepherd reported to Geiger that all organized resistance on Oroku Peninsula had ended.

In summarising the operation, Shepherd wrote:

The ten-day battle was a bitter one, from its inception to the destruction of the last organized resistance. The enemy had taken full advantage of the terrain which adapted itself extraordinarily well to a deliberate defense in depth. The rugged coral outcroppings and the many small precipitous hills had obviously been organized for a defense over a long period of time. Cave and tunnel systems of a most elaborate nature had been cut into each terrain feature of importance, and heavy weapons were sited for defense against attack from any direction.

Despite the powerful converging attack of three regiments, the advance was slow, laborious, and bitterly opposed. The capture of each defensive locality was a problem in itself, involving carefully thought out planning and painstaking execution. During ten days' fighting, almost 5,000 Japanese were killed and nearly 200 taken prisoner. Thirty of our tanks were disabled, many by mines. One tank was destroyed by two direct hits from an 8 inch naval gun fired at point blank range. Finally, 1,608 Marines were killed and wounded.

An outstanding aspect of the Oroku operation was the ability of the Tenth Army to exploit the amphibious capability of one of its Marine divisions during a critical phase of the Okinawa campaign, despite the extremely limited time available for assault prepara-

tions. Overcoming most obstacles and discounting others, the 6th Marine Division planned and launched an amphibious assault within the allotted thirty-six hour period.

While the 6th Division was temporarily out of the Tenth Army line and preparing for the Oroku invasion, the attack to the south had accelerated in momentum and force. By late afternoon of 3rd June, the 7th Infantry Division had reached the east coast below Kakibana to cut off the Chinen Peninsula completely. The US 32nd Infantry then moved into the hill complex of the peninsula to destroy any members of the Japanese garrison still remaining. Major-General Arnold then consolidated the lines of his two other regiments in the hills overlooking Itokazu and Toyama, where his troops poised for an attack to the southwest against Kiyamu Peninsula positions.

To the right of the 7th Division, the 96th Division also scored gains on the 3rd, taking Kamizato, Tero, and then Inasomi without encountering much in the way of resistance. Before halting for the night, this division's

Flame thrower operation against a Japanese cave

assault regiment had taken 1,400 yards of enemy territory, even though the combination of continuing bad weather and almost insurmountable supply problems seemed to conspire against further American successes. The 1st Marine Division also advanced with relative ease, garnering new positions and, yet, seemingly unable to fix and fight an enemy that drifted away to new positions on Kiyamu.

On the day that the 6th Division landed on Oroku, the 1st Division rolled up gains totalling 1,800 yards in its drive south from the Naha-Yonabaru valley line. Del Valle's regiments made this gain despite a faltering supply system that threatened to break down completely in the mud and rain. Like the supply net elsewhere behind the rest of the Tenth Army divisions, the roads in the rear of the 1st Divisions had become such quagmires that even tractors and bulldozers stalled when they attempted to drag division motor transport out of or over the mud. Tracked and wheeled vehicles were unable to cross the Kokuba and the approaches to the bridge at the mouth

of the river were untrafficable for a distance of nearly half a mile. In general, the logistical support of forward units was maintained by individual marines, who hand-carried supplies to dumps behind the lines. In one area, the rain had turned the fields into calf-deep mud wallows in which the men walking in them had the soles of their shoes pulled off by the suction of the ooze. To the relief of all, the rains stopped on the night of 5th-6th June, although the sun was not out long enough on the 6th to begin drying up the roads.

During its drive south, the 1st Marine Division was sporadically halted for brief periods before a number of blocking positions organized and manned by small enemy groups, each of which was generally company-sized. All of them together probably comprised a force equaling no more than two battalions. Under orders to delay the Tenth Army for as long as possible, the tactical situation, however, prevented these Japanese units from setting up anything other than hastily contrived defensive positions which were unable to hold back the aggressive Marine offensive for long.

When reconnaissance patrols uncovered the Japanese strongpoints, infantry commanders deployed their forces to take the objective by a combination of fire and maneuver. In most cases, the major attack force was able to maneuver into position to assault the flanks or rear of the enemy. While units in front of the Japanese position provided fire support to fix the enemy in place, the enveloping element performed its mission. Regardless of the methods employed, del Valle remarked that 'it was refreshing to be able to maneuver again, even on a modest scale'.

Clearing skies on 7th June revealed further American successes, as the 1st Division, now the right flank unit in the IIIAC zone, broke through to the east coast north of Itoman and thus joined the 6th Division in isolating the Okinawa Naval Base Force from the rest of Ushijima's troops in the south. Anticipating many more casualties before the fighting for Okinawa ended, a landing strip for the artillery-spotting Grasshoppers was placed into operation approximately 2,000 yards north of Itoman on 11th June. Now casualties could be flown almost directly from front-line medical clearing stations to hospitals in the rear, a distance of twelve miles, in eight minutes on the average. This brief flight obviated a long and often body-racking haul in an ambulance jeep over roads that were such in name only.

On 11th June also, the 7th Marines advanced 400-1,000 yards against ever-stiffening enemy opposition. After the village of Tera was cleared to gain the high ground to the south, the regiment faced Kunishi Ridge, which was to be 'the scene of the most frantic, bewildering, and costly close-in battle on the southern tip of Okinawa.'

Running from the northeast to the southwest for a distance of perhaps 1,500 yards, the sheer coral escarpment named Kunishi Ridge held enemy positions which comprised the western anchor of the last heavily defended line in front of Kiyamu. Both the forward and reverse slopes of this ridge were replete with caves, weapons emplacements, and fortified tombs, all of which reinforced natural defenses provided by the complex and difficult terrain features of the ridge itself. In front of the 7th Marines line, a broad valley containing grassy meadows and rice paddies led to this crag and afforded the defenders unobstructed lanes of fire and the attackers little cover and concealment. Approaching tanks would fare no better than the infantry since the armor was restricted to two roads leading into the objective area – both covered extremely well by Japanese antitank guns. One route followed the coast line, while the second one cut across the center of the ridge at right angles, dividing it.

Having pushed through Itoman and Tera on the morning of the 11th, the two 7th Marines battalions in the assault prepared to continue on to Kunishi Ridge. At 1400, two hours after the attack began, enfilading fire from Hill 69, beyond the ridge, forced the assault to a standstill.

Because of this fire and that coming from Yuza Dake in the 96th Division zone, the 7th Marines commander, Colonel Edward W Snedeker, decided that it would be too costly to continue a daylight attack and he ordered the assault units to withdraw. After making an aerial reconnaissance of the ridge in a low-flying observation plane, he concluded that a night attack would be likely to succeed.

That afternoon, as the assault battalions dug in a night defense and prepared to continue their push the next day, the two assault battalion commanders and their staffs were thoroughly oriented and briefed on the general scheme of maneuver for the night attack. Snedeker decided to drive straight across the valley, using the road leading into the ridge separating the battalion zones and the telephone poles bordering the road as a guide. The assault elements were to penetrate the enemy defenses at the point where the road entered the ridge. There, the battalions would peel off to their respective zones of attack and roll up the enemy's line. Until the hour of attack, 0330 on 12th June, normal artillery fire was to be placed alternately on Kunishi Ridge and then Mezado Ridge – 500 to 600 yards south of Kunishi – and thereafter only on the latter. In order to maintain deception and guarantee that the enemy would be surprised, the division ordered that use of flares and illumination of any kind was prohibited – except in cases of emergency – after 0245 on the morning of the attack.

Before the 7th Marines push began, the Tenth Army decided to induce the enemy to surrender. Prior to and following the L-Day landings, the Japanese on Okinawa had been subjected to a massive psychological warfare effort in which propaganda leaflets were delivered by aircraft drops and artillery shells. Also, Japanese-language broadcasts were directed at the enemy over loudspeakers placed near the front lines. For a period of several days before 11th June, this war of paper and

**Even a mechanized army needs muscle:
6th Division Marines manhandle a
howitzer behind the battle lines**

words had been accelerated, emphasizing the hopelessness of the Japanese position and the futility of continued fighting. Both the leaflets and the broadcasts called upon Ushijima to surrender.

On the afternoon of the 11th, Buckner sent a Tenth Army parley team, fully empowered to negotiate a truce with any authorized Japanese party, to the 2/7 observation post overlooking Itoman. At 1700, all firing ceased in the 7th Marines zone in dubious but hopeful anticipation of a favorable enemy response to the words spoken over the loudspeakers. While no official party bearing white flags appeared, six enemy soldiers surrendered about an hour later to the Marines in the lines. The battlefield's unnatural silence was shattered about 1804, when hostile mortar fire fell on the parley team, and American artillery resumed fire on Kunishi in answer.

Ushijima did not receive the surrender message until a week later, on 17th June. Yahara later reported that this was the normal amount of time required for a message to be passed to the rear at this stage of the fighting. Upon delivery of the Buckner communique, 'Cho and Ushijima both laughed and declared that, as *Samurai*, it would not be consonant with their honor to entertain such a proposal.'

As scheduled, the night attack jumped off at 0330 on the 12th, and by 0500 reached the crest of the ridge, achieving complete surprise – to the point of destroying several small enemy groups caught while they prepared their breakfasts. At daybreak, heavy Japanese fire caught other Marine units moving through the valley to reinforce those already on the ridge. It became painfully apparent that the Japanese on the ridge had recovered quickly from their initial setback. As del Valle described the situation facing the 7th Marines at the end of the day, it 'was one of the tactical oddities of this peculiar warfare. We were *on* the ridge, the Japs were *in* it, both on the forward and reverse slopes.'

In the four days following its initial attack on Kunishi Ridge, the 7th Marines was almost completely isolated from other friendly ground units by 'No Man's Valley,' the 800-yard approach to its positions. This broad expanse was thoroughly covered by the fire of Japanese soldiers infesting the lower slopes and crests flanking the ridge. Supplies were either dropped by parachute or brought in by tanks. Some air drops fell in the valley, but they were in the minority. The rest fell right on target, in a drop zone controlled by the Marines. Sometimes it was dangerous for the Americans to recover supply containers in these supposedly safe areas because of the many enemy snipers awaiting such targets of opportunity. One Japanese sharpshooter alone killed and wounded twenty-two Marines before he was finally located and eliminated.

During the course of the fight to hold and occupy Kunishi Ridge, 1st Division tanks were employed in missions to carry supplies and personnel up to 7th Marines positions and to evacuate casualties on the return trip. By displacing the assistant driver of each tank it was possible to cram six riflemen inside the Shermans. Despite the inviting targets their sheer bulk offered, the tanks did yeoman work in bringing out the wounded, some of whom were strapped to the sides of the mediums and then sandbagged as protection against enemy fire.

In face of continuous Japanese attempts to dislodge them from their tenuous hold on Kunishi, the 7th Marines held. To the left, the 1st Marines on the corps boundary had entered Ozato on 12th June against only slight opposition in contrast to the fighting on Kunishi. On the following day, patrols from the 1st began reconnoitering towards that portion of the ridge in its zone in preparation for their predawn attack scheduled for the 14th. While all efforts in the 1st Division zone on the 13th were concentrated on supporting the new attack, the incessant cannonading of artillery and naval gunfire gave Ushijima's forces no respite in the southern part of the island. LCI gunboats mounting 4.5-inch rockets took positions off the tip of Southern Okinawa to rake reverse slope defenses of the Thirty-second Army

unmercifully. More than 500 rockets ripped into the towns of Makabe and Komesu in an hour's time alone.

H-Hour for the 1st Marines attack on Kunishi Ridge was 0330 on the 14th. Following a thirty minute artillery preparation, the assault battalion moved out with two companies in the van. By 0500, two platoons of the leading company had reached the topographical crest of the ridge, while the remainder of the company was stopped well below this point by extremely heavy and accurate enemy fire. At daybreak, increasingly active Japanese sniper and supporting arms fire on the flanks and rear of the assault companies isolated them from the rest of the battalion. Tanks then lumbered forward to serve the Marines in this portion of Kunishi in the same manner as they had supported the 7th Marines earlier.

The efforts of the 2/1 assault companies notwithstanding, they still had not taken more than seventy-five yards of the ridge when 2/5 relieved them after dark on 15th June. Earlier that day, 3/5 had relieved 1/1, at which time the 5th Marines officially assumed responsibility for the

Marines follow up behind explosive charges used to destroy Japanese defences

former zone of the 1st Marines.

On the day before these fresh troops joined the fight for Kunishi, the 7th Marines had resumed its grinding advance, by 'the slow, methodical destruction of enemy emplacements on the ridge, to which the descriptive word "processing" has come to be applied.' In the face of difficult terrain and an unrelenting enemy opposition, elements of the 7th Marines succeeded in closing to the outskirts of Kunishi village beyond the ridge.

During 15th and 16th June, naval gunfire, rockets, artillery, air, and 81mm mortars pounded the enemy from afar without let-up, while both gun and flame tanks furnished close-in direct support fire. This was all to no avail, for this hail of steel was unable to make an impression on Japanese defenses as the 7th Marines attempted to move beyond Kunishi to the next division objective, the Mezado Hill mass. By the end of 16th June, however, Kunishi Ridge was no longer a major obstacle in the way of the 1st Division, for the terrain that the Japanese had so doggedly defended here, including the approaches to Mezado, had been cleaned out. Only that portion of the ridge in the 5th Marines zone still presented some problems, but they were slowly surmounted by dint of sheer courage and overwhelming fire support.

As 1st Division troops prepared for the final drive to the south, mopping up operations on Oroku Peninsula ended, and Shepherd's staff drew up plans for eventual commitment of the division in the IIIAC line, again on the right. Initially, the 22nd Marines would pass through the right flank elements of the 7th Marines on 17th June. An uneventful passage of the lines took place at 0300 and by dawn, 6th Division assault units were in jump-off positions at the base of the northern slope of Mezado

Okinawan civilians under guard

Ridge, prepared to attack in coordination with 3/7 on the left. By noon, the highest point on the ridge had been taken and the momentum of the attack carried the assault battalion, 3/22, through the village of Mezado as well. Before dusk, this battalion had captured the key terrain around Hill 69, 400 yards south of Mezado, and was in position to attack the next major objective, Kuwanga Ridge, the next day.

When 1st Division troops attacked on the 17th, their objective was another hill also designated Hill 69, east of Mezado. Following an unopposed 1,400-yard drive across the plateau just east of Mezado to seize both Hills 69 and 52 – the latter about 110 yards to the southeast of the former – the attacking Marines halted for a short time to reorganize and then attempted to continue the drive to the crest of Hill 79, the last remaining barrier before Makabe. Heavy Japanese fire from positions on the

high ground commanding the Kuwanga-Makabe road forced the battalion in the lead to halt for the night before it could win the hill. Once dug in, the Marines quickly organized their defenses to block all enemy attempts to infiltrate and counterattack in the darkness.

When a Japanese counterattack was finally mounted that night, it was directed against 1/22, located in Mezado proper. This determined enemy effort, born of despair, was doomed from its inception because that portion of the Japanese 22nd Regiment scheduled to exploit the counterattack had been almost completely destroyed in the fighting that afternoon. In effect, the near annihilation of the 22nd Regiment meant that the left flank of the Japanese outpost line had all but collapsed and that the enemy units holding positions near Makabe were faced with the threat of having their left flank rolled up.

Geiger's divisions were prepared to take advantage of the situation with the infusion of new troops into the battle on the next day, 18th June. While the 7th Marines finished 'processing' Kunishi Ridge, the 8th Marines of the 2nd Marine Division prepared to reinforce the 1st Marine Division and to help in the attack to the southern tip of Okinawa. This fresh unit had returned to Saipan with its parent division after participating in the feint landings on the southeastern coast of Okinawa on L-Day. Although the division was released from the Tenth Army on 14th May, the 8th Marines remained under Buckner's control to be employed in landings on Iheya Shima, fifteen miles northwest of the northern tip of Okinawa, and Aguni Shima, thirty miles west of Okinawa.

Because of the heavy damage that the fleet, and especially the radar pickets, had sustained in the *Kamikaze* raids, Turner was anxious to develop long-range radar and fighter-director facilities on the outlying islands of Okinawa Gunto. Resulting from a study that the Tenth Army prepared, it was decided that Tori, Aguni, Iheya, and Kume Shimas could be captured, in that order. A reinforced company from the 165th Infantry made an unopposed landing on Tori on 12th May, and a detachment from Marine Air Warning Squadron 1 began operations almost immediately thereafter.

Since the battle to take Okinawa was now reaching a crucial stage, Buckner did not believe that the forces already committed in the fight to the south could or should be diverted to such secondary missions as the landings on the small islands noted above. He then requested that the 8th Marines specifically be returned to Okinawa for employment in the Iheya-Aguni landings. In the course of his inspection of the 2nd Marine Division on Saipan in February, he had visited the 8th Marines and inspected the regimental quarters and galleys. It seemed to one observer accompanying Buckner on this visit that the 8th Marines had made a tremendous impression on the Tenth Army commander, and that he had been particularly impressed with the battalion commanders. Buckner later told his Marine Deputy Chief of Staff that 'he had never before had the privilege of meeting such an alert group . . .' It is perhaps for this reason that the 8th Marines was selected for the landings. Unfortunately, Buckner's strange fascination with this Marine rifle regiment was to prove fatal.

The 2nd and 3rd Battalions of the 8th Marines landed on Iheya on 3rd June to find neither enemy troops nor opposition. The Marines encountered only 3,000 confused but docile natives, who were taken into tow by military government teams of the Tenth Army Island Command. The island was declared secure the next day. The landing on Aguni Shima was delayed by bad weather until 9th June, when 1/8 went ashore on the island under circumstances similar to those experienced at Iheya. In accordance with Tenth Army instructions received before these two minor operations were mounted, the 8th Marines stood ready for immediate commitment on Okinawa upon completion of the landings. When fresh units were needed for the final thrust against the Japanese dug in on Kiyamu Peninsula, the 8th Marines was available.

The end of an army

By 4th June, the remnants of the Thirty-second Army had fully manned the outpost line of Kiyamu Peninsula. 'Attrition during retirement operations,' was the official Japanese explanation for the 20,000-man differential between Ushijima's estimated strength figure of 51,000 men in late May, and the total number of effectives available at the beginning of June.

Of Ushijima's remaining forces in the lines, approximately twenty percent were survivors of the original, first-rate infantry and artillery defense garrison; the rest were either untrained rear-echelon personnel or the *Boeitai*. Leading this motly force at battalion level and above were many of the original senior commanders who had remained alive and were still capable of arousing a fighting spirit in their men.

Their unflagging belief in a final Japanese victory was unrealistic in view of the alarming losses of weapons and equipment that the Thirty-second Army had sustained since L-Day. Despite outward signs of imminent defeat and their impoverished condition, the confidence that Ushijima's army had in their ultimate victory was derived from deep-seated tradition, strongly enforced discipline, and the historically pervasive influence of Japanese military doctrine throughout the Empire. These intangibles, almost completely alien and incomprehensible to the Americans, promised that Kiyamu Peninsula was not to fall and the battle for Okinawa was not to end before a final, violent climax.

Influenced by the location and relative strength of enemy strongpoints facing the Tenth Army, and the availability and status of his assault forces, Buckner had shifted the boundary between the XXIV and III Amphibious Corps west on 4th June. In Geiger's now narrower zone, the 6th Marine Division had captured Oroku Peninsula, while the 1st Marine Division attended to its tasks of cutting off the peninsula from the rest of Ushijima's army, capturing Itoman, seizing Kunishi and Mezado Ridges, and then driving to Ara Saki, the southernmost point of the island. The assignments which

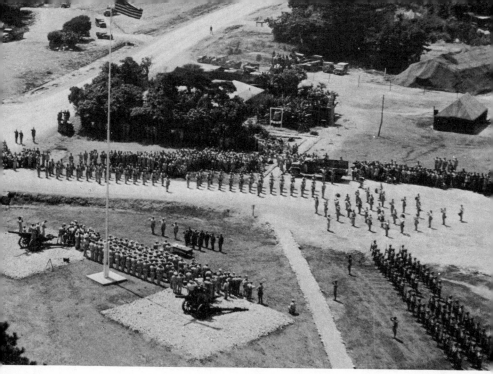

Hodges' corps faced were no less difficult, for they included the capture of the Yuza Dake-Yaeju Dake Escarpment, as a primary objective. On line facing this impressive terrain feature were the 7th and 96th Divisions.

Nearly two weeks of punishing and brutal fighting ensued before these two Army divisions could eliminate all Japanese resistance in this area. XXIV Corps units spent the period 4th-8th June regrouping and attempting to gain favorable jump-off positions for the attack on the escarpment, which was scheduled for the 9th. All supporting arms were employed to soften up the well-organized enemy defense system. Armored flamethrower, tank, assault gun, and artillery fire added to the point-blank blasts of experimental 57mm and 75mm recoilless rifles, which had been recently developed and sent to Okinawa for test firing under combat conditions.

The defense of the Yuza Dake-Yaeju Dake outpost line had been assigned to two units. Guarding the escarpment from Hill 95 on the east coast

to Yaeju Dake was the seemingly indestructible 44th Independent Mixed Brigade. Defense of the remainder of the high ground, including Yuza Dake, was the responsibility of the 24th Division. Added to the fanatic, last-ditch determination of the Japanese forces here was the natural, fortress-like features of the terrain they defended. This combination enabled only one regiment, the 89th, to defend the Yuza Dake area.

Facing the 7th Division were enemy troops who compared unfavorably with the veterans defending Yuza Dake. Coming from miscellaneous shipping engineer, sea raiding, mortar, and line of communication outfits, the soldiers were loosely organized into provisional infantry regiments and put into the 44th IMB line. The vital Hill 95 – Hangusuku-Nakaza Valley area was held by tired troops which first began to give way under the repeated pounding in the initial 7th Division advance. The Americans relentlessly pushed forward on 11th June, the second day of the corps-wide attack on the escarpment, and threatened the rest of the

Thirty-second Army line by breaking into the 44th IMB defenses. An attempt by Ushijima to shore up this section of his rapidly crumbling outpost by committing loosely organized infantry units proved to be 'as ineffective as throwing water on parched soil.'

Clear weather on 13th June, following a night of abortive enemy counterattacks, permitted XXIV Corps to employ all supporting arms on the enemy in front of its troops. Japanese reinforcements attempting to reach the front were blasted by American air, naval gunfire, and artillery. Although the 89th Regiment, reinforced now, still maintained its hold on Yuza Dake, its rear and flank were threatened by the impending Tenth Army penetration south of Yaeju Dake.

Elsewhere, as Japanese positions began to give way under the pressure of the savage American onslaught, Thirty-second Army headquarters lost all contact with the last infantry element of the 44th IMB to maintain unit integrity. To stave off the last stages of a crushing defeat, Ushijima ordered the 62nd Division into the deteriorating line from its reserve positions southwest of Makabe, but a murderous lashing from American supporting arms thoroughly disrupted the deployment, with the net result that few, if any, of the enemy troops arrived at their destination.

The 96th Division took advantage of this confused enemy situation to rush its infantry through the Yuza Dake perimeter. On the left flank of the Tenth Army, the 7th Division surged down the coast, and by the end of 17th June, XXIV Corps regiments held firm control of all commanding ground on the escarpment. Compressed between the front lines of the Army corps and the southernmost point of Okinawa was all that was left of the Thirty-second Army, a hodge-podge of units and individuals. Before the island was to be secured by the Tenth Army, most of these Japanese troops would die violently in a forlorn attempt to defend Ushijima's headquarters.

As the Tenth Army advanced against now steadily lessened resistance on 18th June, the death throes of the Ushijima force became quite obvious. Although most sections of the Japanese line proved softer than before, two isolated centers of opposition developed during the day – one around Medeera, and the other in the area of Mabuni. The first was held by the 24th Division, and the second, in the vicinity of Hill 89, was defended by elements of the headquarters and troops of remaining Thirty-second Army units.

Leading the 1st Marine Division attack on the 18th was the 8th Marines, which had relieved the 7th Marines the previous night. At 0730, the assault battalion jumped off from Mezado Ridge to head south and occupy a line west of Makabe from which it could launch a quick, decisive thrust to the sea. To cap its first day in the lines, this 8th Marines unit made a rapid advance of 1,400 yards against sporadic machine gun, mortar, and artillery fire. Early on the 18th, Buckner had gone forward to witness the fighting, and 'probably chose the 1st Division front on this date because he wanted to see the 8th Marines in action . . .' On his way to the front, Buckner met Colonel Harold C Roberts, commander of the 22nd Marines, who urged the Tenth Army commander not to proceed further because there was considerable flanking fire coming from positions facing the 96th Division. Buckner failed to to heed this advice and continued on. An hour or so later, Roberts was killed by sniper fire on another part of the front.

The Tenth Army commander went to a ridge where 3/8 had set up an observation post, and where he could observe tank-infantry operations ahead. He took a position behind two coral boulders separated by a slit through which he could see the action in front of him. Within minutes, a Japanese 47mm antitank shell hit the base of the boulders, followed by five more shells in rapid succession. Either a shell fragment or a piece of coral hit Buckner in the chest, mortally wounding him, and he died soon afterwards.

Upon being informed of his commander's death, the Tenth Army Chief of Staff reported the event to

Nimitz, and, knowing Buckner's expressed desires regarding the succession of command, recommended in the message that Geiger be designated the new Tenth Army commander. On 19th June, Geiger was promoted to lieutenant-general and officially appointed Commanding General, Tenth Army, the same day. This was the first time, to that date, that a Marine officer had commanded a unit of this size. General Joseph W Stilwell, USA, former Deputy Commander of the Southeast Asia Command, arrived on Okinawa on 23rd June, relieving Geiger the same day, only after the Marine general had successfully directed the final combat operations on Okinawa.

Early in the morning on the day that General Buckner was killed, the 5th Marines attacked to take Hill 79, northwest of Makabe, and by noon the regimental objective was secured, but not before a coordinated tank-infantry assault was thrown at the defenders. By the end of the day, the 6th Division also had made important gains, and at dark was in possession of Kuwanga Ridge. In

The campaign lost, many Japanese surrender despite the *Bushido* code

the XXIV Corps zone, the 96th Division made an attack on Medeera positions from the east in coordination with a 1st Marine Division assault on the same objective from the west; the 7th Division, at the same time, continued its drive. In a two-pronged attack, the Army unit sent one assault element down the reverse slope of Hill 153 to sweep past Medeera and end its drive at the corps boundary near Komesu. The second prong of the attack was mounted by three battalions abreast advancing slowly down the coast towards Mabuni and the Thirty-second Army headquarters.

Fully realizing that 'his Army's fate had been sealed,' Ushijima began spiritual and physical preparations for a *Samurai's* death. On 16th June, he sent the first of several farewell messages, this one a moving report to Imperial General Headquarters in Tokyo, which read:

'With a burning desire to destroy the arrogant enemy, the men in my command have fought the invaders for almost three months. We have failed to crush the enemy, despite our death-defying resistance, and now we are doomed.

Since taking over this island, our forces have, with the devoted support of the local population, exerted every effort to build up defenses. Since the enemy landing, our air and land forces, working in concert, have done everything possible to defend the island.

To my regret we are no longer able to continue the fight. For this failure I tender deepest apologies to the emperor and the people of the homeland . . . I pray for the souls of men killed in battle and for the prosperity of the Imperial Family.

Death will not quell the desire of my spirit to defend the homeland.

With deepest appreciation of the kindness and cooperation of my superiors and colleagues in arms, I bid farewell to you forever.
Mitsuru Ushijima.'

Three days later, Ushijima sent a last message to all Thirty-second Army units with which he still had contact. He congratulated the survivors on having performed their 'assigned mission in a manner which leaves nothing to regret' and called upon them 'to fight to the last and die for the eternal cause of loyalty to the Emperor.' He then directed most of his staff officers to disguise themselves as island natives, leave the command post, and infiltrate the Tenth Army lines in order to escape to northern Okinawa. Some of his key advisors, like Yahara, were directed to try to reach Japan in order to report to Imperial General Headquarters. And still others were ordered to organize guerrilla warfare activities in the rear of Tenth Army tactical units.

Despite their thorough indoctrination in the tenets of Japanese military tradition, there were some enemy soldiers who did not particularly care to die for Emperor and Homeland. Under the direction of American psychological warfare teams, interpreters and cooperative prisoners broadcast inducements to surrender over loudspeakers mounted on tanks operating at the 7th Division front

and on LCIs cruising off the southern coast of the island. Three thousand civilians were convinced to surrender, and beginning 19th June, a number of enemy soldiers and *Boeitai* lay down their arms and gave up in the face of the 7th Division advance. At this stage of the campaign, the broadcasts influenced increasing numbers of the enemy to surrender as the conviction that all was lost and their cause was hopeless sank into their war-weary minds.

With their progress now slowed to a walking pace by civilians fleeing to the north through the lines as well as by heavy resistance put up by a well-entrenched enemy, 7th Division troops, nevertheless, advanced to within 200 yards of the outskirts of Mabuni by nightfall of 19th June. Tanks accompanying the infantry placed direct fire on caves fronting Hill 89 at the very time that Ushijima was giving a farewell party for his departing staff officers.

On the right of the 7th Division zone, infantry elements drove towards Medeera from the south and east against considerably weakened resistance and fire. Small fanatic groups defending the complex terrain around the 24th Division headquarters, nevertheless, had to be overcome before Medeera itself could be taken. Northwest of Medeera, 96th Division troops pushing towards Aragachi from the north found the same Japanese reluctance to withdraw being experienced in several other places on the front. While observing the efforts of his division to gain the heights overlooking Aragachi, Brigadier-General Claudius M Easely, Assistant Division Commander of the 96th, was killed by enemy machine gun fire.

In the IIIAC zone, the 8th Marines completely penetrated Japanese defenses in the vicinity of Komesu to reach the sea. Less successful, however, were the day-long efforts of the 5th Marines to take Hills 79 and 81, northeast and north of Makabe, respectively. The 6th Division, with the 22nd Marines on the west coast and the 4th Marines pacing the attack of the 8th Marines on the division boundary, advanced rapidly towards the tip of the island, but the Kiyamu-Gusuku hill mass prevented the 4th from reaching the coast on 19th June.

The next day, the 29th Marines advanced to the coast, tied in with the 4th Marines for the night, and thus barred the way to enemy attempting to escape to the sea. Psychological warfare teams again went into action on 20th June, broadcasting surrender messages from LCIs in the waters off southern Okinawa. A feeling that further resistance was futile as well as a sense of impending doom impelled some 4,000 civilians and 800 soldiers to heed the message and leave their inaccessible cave refuges lining the coastal cliffs.

The 1st and 2nd Battalions of the 5th Marines spent 20th June again attempting to reduce the seemingly impregnable Hills 79 and 81, with only heavy casualties and no gains to show for their efforts. To the left, in the XXIV Corps zone, only two strong enemy pockets remained this day. One was centered about the caves holding Ushijima's headquarters, and the second was in Medeera and west of the village on Hills 79 and 85, which, together with Hill 81 in the 1st Division zone, formed Makabe Ridge. The last courier contact between the two strongpoints was made on the night of 20th June, after the commander of the 24th Division, General Amamiya, urged his soldiers 'to fight to the last man in their present positions.'

This exhortation fell on ears that could no longer hear, for the general had few troops alive to defend the Medeera sector at this time. The only soldiers he had left comprised a mixed bag of artillerists, drivers, medical attendants, engineers, *Boei-tai*, and personnel from almost every headquarters unit of the forces that

Military honors for Lieutenant-General Simon B Buckner, Tenth Army Commander, killed in the fighting

had made up the island garrison on L-Day. Despite the constantly increasing number of Japanese soldiers surrendering, and others who were committing suicide, the Tenth Army still had to contend with some enemy troops who were determined to fight to the last. An attack to destroy these hold-outs on Makabe Ridge was scheduled for noon of 21st June.

At 1027 that day, Shepherd reported to his corps commander that organized resistance had ended in the 6th Division zone. After some minor mopping up operations during the 21st, Company G, 2/22, raised the division colors on the southernmost point of the island in its zone that afternoon. This feat thus duplicated its accomplishment earlier in the campaign when it was the unit to raise the same colors over the northernmost point of Okinawa.

In the remainder of the IIIAC zone, the 7th and 8th Marines flushed out enemy hold-outs and accepted the surrender of ever-increasing numbers of soldiers and civilians. At 1735, Hill 79 was finally taken, but to 2/5, Hill 81 proved a harder nut to crack as it attacked once more at 1104. The effort to secure the objective was spurred on by information – later proved false – that this was the last organized enemy position on Okinawa. After several unsuccessful attempts to gain the hill, the battalion was reinforced by 3/5, whose commander assumed joint command of the two battalions in the attack. At 1700, all assault companies reported their portion of the objective secured, and organized resistance in the III Amphibious Corps zone thus ended.

In the XXIV Corps zone, heavy fighting throughout the 21st marked the Army drive to seize Makabe Ridge, which was finally taken at 1730. But before Hodges could report his zone secured, his troops had to come to grips with a bitterly held, last-ditch Japanese defense. Objectives were captured only after enemy defenders were killed literally to the last man. XXIV Corps troops first secured Mabuni, then Hill 89. Buckner's 'corkscrew and blowtorch' tactics were effectively employed by flame tanks and demolition teams burning and blasting the 'palace guard' defending the cave entrances to the Thirty-second Army command post. By the end of this last day of the Okinawa campaign, Hill 89 had been secured and its former defenders were frantically attempting to escape a horrible death by entombment. It was surprising that there were any Japanese alive in the vicinity of Hill 89 at this stage of the battle. Earlier in the month, TAF pilots had discovered this scene of enemy activity and had made it a prime target. For instance, on 13th June, a total of sixty-four Corsairs had burned and blasted the hill and its vicinity with 124 napalm bombs and 335 5-inch rockets in less than an hour's time.

After eighty-two days of bloody and bitter endeavor, the rapid advance of the Tenth Army in the final stages of the campaign brought about the irrevocable collapse of all major Japanese opposition. Thus Geiger could announce at 1305 on 21st June that the island of Okinawa had been secured by American forces that day. The official end of the Okinawa campaign was marked by a formal flag-raising ceremony at Tenth Army headquarters on 22nd June, attended by representatives from all units of the Iceberg command. The Deputy Chief of Staff of the Tenth Army read the official message declaring the end of organized resistance on the island, and Geiger then gave the order for the flag to be raised.

On this same day, Ushijima ended his life in accordance with the dictates that governed his living of it – the traditional way of the *Samurai*. His decision had been made on the day before, as he saw that his defenses had been overrun and his forces shattered, and that there was little hope of forestalling the inevitable fate of the Thirty-second Army. Joining him in fulfilling his obligation to the Emperor and dying in the symbolic way of *Bushido* was his chief of staff, Cho.

At noon on 22nd June, Ushijima dressed himself in his full field uniform and Cho put on a white kimono on which he had written, 'The offering of one's life is to fulfil the duties towards the Emperor and the country. Cho, Isamu.' The two led a party of aides and staff officers out to a ledge at the mouth of the cave headquarters, and ten minutes later, first Ushijima and then Cho died as they each committed *hara-kiri*. As each bared his abdomen to the knife used in the ceremonial disembowelment and thrust inward, there was a shout and the flash of a sword as the headquarters adjutant decapitated first one general and then the other. The bodies were then secretly buried in graves prepared beforehand at the foot of the cliff of Hill 89.

On 25th June, Imperial General Headquarters announced the end of Japanese operations on Okinawa, and, in effect, of the Thirty-second Army. IGHQ then put all of its efforts into defensive preparations to secure the Home Islands against an anticipated American invasion, which was believed not too far in the future.

Although the commander and chief of staff, as well as many other officers and men of the Thirty-second Army were dead, and others surrendering in droves, still other Japanese soldiers – both individually and in groups – continued to hold out. To safeguard the Island Command forces undertaking a mass base development program to convert Okinawa into a staging base for further operations against Japan, Stilwell ordered the Tenth Army to begin an intensive, coordinated mop-up of southern Okinawa on 23rd June. The American sweep northwards was made by the five divisions that had made the final drive in the south and were on line when the campaign ended. They began the sweep by merely making an about-face in position. Seven days later, the operation was successfully completed, with an estimated 8,975 Japanese killed and another 3,800 taken prisoner.

Enemy losses for the Okinawa campaign were placed at 107,539 counted dead and an estimated 23,764 assumed to have been sealed in caves or buried by the Japanese themselves. A total of 10,755 were captured or gave themselves up. As the overall Japanese casualty rate of 142,058 was 'far above a reasonable estimate of military strength on the island,' Tenth Army intelligence agencies presumed that approximately 42,000

of these casualties were civilians who had been unfortunately killed or wounded in American artillery, naval gunfire, and air attacks on enemy troops and installations while the natives were in their vicinity.

American losses were heavy also. The total reported Tenth Army casualty figures were 7,374 killed or died of wounds, 31,807 wounded or injured in action, and 230 missing. In addition, there were 26,221 non-battle casualties. Both British and American naval forces sustained heavy casualties while supporting and maintaining the Tenth Army. During the eighty-two days of ground operations, thirty-four ships and craft of various types were sunk and 368 damaged; 763 carrier-based aircraft were lost as a result of combat and operational accidents. In addition, 4,907 sailors were killed or missing in action, and 4,824 were wounded. At the time that these losses were sustained, ships' and ground antiaircraft fire and Navy-controlled or coordinated planes destroyed 7,830 Japanese aircraft and sixteen combat ships.

Shortly after the initial landings on Okinawa, British observers accompanying the Iceberg force reported that, 'This operation was the most audacious and complex enterprise which has yet been undertaken by the American Amphibious Forces . . .' And they were undoubtedly right, for 'more ships were used, more troops put ashore, more supplies transported, more naval guns fired against shore targets' than in any previous campaign in the Pacific War. Despite the immensity of all of the factors involved in the Iceberg operation, the Okinawa campaign realistically demonstrated the soundness of the fundamental amphibious doctrine developed by the Marine Corps and the Navy over the years, and which they had tempered in the hard fighting in the Pacific. If there had been no amphibious warfare doctrine developed in the prewar period because of the failure of this tactic at Gallipoli, despite the ineptitude with which it had been employed, then some other new strategy would have undoubtedly been devised to capture Japanese-held islands in the Pacific. It is difficult to imagine, however, any tactic other than an amphibious assault which, under the circumstances, could have accomplished the job as satisfactorily. Reinforcing this thesis is a statement made by Geiger, who pointed out that the landing on and battle for Okinawa 'reemphasized most clearly that our basic principles of tactics and techniques are sound, "in the book", and need only to be followed in combat.'

The touchstone to success at Okinawa was interservice cooperation, where 'Army artillery supported Marine infantry and vice versa,' and where 'Marine and Army planes were used interchangeably and operated under the same tactical command,' and 'each contiguous infantry unit was mutually supporting and interdependent,' and, finally, when 'the Navy's participation was vital to both throughout.'

Teamwork was a most important ingredient in the formula for reduction of the heavily fortified Japanese positions. During the course of the Okinawa campaign, the work of supporting arms, infantry-engineer, air-ground, and tank-infantry teams played a vital role in the defeat of the enemy. Ground assault operations, however, were the special province of the armored and infantry units. Concerning the armored support of his 6th Division Marines, Shepherd wrote, 'if any one supporting arm can be singled out as having contributed more than any others during the progress of the campaign, the tank would certainly be selected.' In a battle lesson issued to his Thirty-second Army, Ushijima supported this theme, stating that 'the enemy's power lies in his tanks. It has become obvious that our general battle against the American forces is a battle against their . . . tanks.'

The story of the Okinawa campaign is incomplete without a brief investigation of Japanese tactics. Contrary to the Japanese beachhead defense doctrine encountered in earlier Pacific landings, the Tenth Army met a resistance in depth similar to that experienced by Americans in the Philippines invasion. From the time that the Iceberg force landed over the Hagushi beaches until it came up

Stars and Stripes over Shuri: a battered Japanese flagpole now bears the conqueror's banner

against the northern outposts of the Shuri line, it was harassed, harried, and delayed by small provisional units and somewhat stronger blocking forces comprised of veteran regulars.

The rugged and complex ridgelines in the Shuri area were defended from vast entrenchments, from a wide variety of fortified caves employed as pillboxes, and from elaborate, multistoried weapons positions that had been gouged out of the ridges and hills and connected by tunnels which usually opened on reverse slopes. 'The continued development and improvement of cave warfare was the most outstanding feature of the enemy's tactics on Okinawa.' Despite the obvious fact that the Thirty-second Army was decisively beaten, Ushijima must be credited with having successfully accomplished his assigned mission. He did provide Japan with valuable time to continue working on the defense of the homeland, but the dropping of atomic bombs on Hiroshima and Nagasaki cancelled out all these efforts.

The final act of the Okinawa story unfolded on 7th September 1945, when Stilwell negotiated the surrender of enemy garrisons in the Ryukyus. Responding to orders issued by Stilwell, senior Japanese commanders reported at the headquarters of the Ryukuus Command – as the Tenth Army had been redesignated – to sign 'unconditional surrender documents representing the complete capitulation of the Ryukyu Islands and over 105,000 Army and Navy forces.' Witnessing the ten minute ceremony were Army and Marine infantry units and tank platoons, while above it all, hundreds of planes flashed by. As the next to last giant step leading to the defeat of Japan, the Okinawa invasion was a prime example of a successful amphibious operation, and the culmination of all that Americans had learned in the Pacific War in the art of mounting a seaborne assault against an enemy-held land mass. This knowledge was to serve well in preparing for the invasion of Japan.

Bibliography

Okinawa: The Last Battle – The War in the Pacific – US Army in World War II Roy E Appleman et al (History Division, Department of the Army, Washington)
History of the Sixth Marine Division Bevan G Cass, ed. (Infantry Journal Press, Washington)
Amphibious Operations – Capture of Okinawa, 27 March – 21 June 1945 (Op Nav 34 -P-07000) Chief of Naval operations. Department of the Navy (Government Printing Office, Washington)
Matterhorn to Nagasaki – The Army Air Forces in World War II Vol 5 Wesley Frank Craven and James Lea Cate (Chicago University Press, Chicago)
The Deadeyes: The Story of the 96th Infantry Division Orlando R Davidson et al (Infantry Journal Press, Washington)
Victory and Occupation – History of US Marine Corps Operations in World War II Vol V Benis M Frank and Henry I Shaw, Jr (Historical Branch, G-3 Division, Headquarters, US Marine Corps, Washington)
Dai Toa Senso Zenshi (The Complete History of the Greater East Asia War), vol IV (Matsu Publishing Company, Tokyo)
Kogun Saburo Hayashi and Alvin D Coox (Marine Corps Association, Quantico)
*The Divine Wind: Japan's Kamikaze Force in World War II Captain Rikihei Inoguchi and Commander Tadashi Nakajima with Roger Pineau (United States Naval Institute, Annapolis)
US Marines and Amphibious War Jeter A Isely and Philip A Crowl (Princeton University Press, Princeton)
The 27th Infantry Division in World War II Captain Edmund G Love (Infantry Journal Press, Washington)
The Old Breed: A History of the First Marine Division in World War II George McMillan (Infantry Journal Press, Washington)
Victory in the Pacific, 1915 – History of United States Naval Operations in World War II vol XIV Samuel Eliot Morison (Little, Brown and Co, Boston)
Ours to Hold it High Lieutenant -Colonel Max Myers (Infantry Journal Press, Washington)
Purnell's History of the Second World War (London)
History of Marine Corps Aviation in World War II Robert Sherrod (Combat Forces Press, Washington)
Handbook on Japanese Military Forces (TM-E-30-480) (United States Army, War Department, Washington)
Official records of units involved in the ICEBERG operation and all correspondence and interviews with participants, all available in the Historical Archives, Headquarters, US Marine Corps, Washington, DC.
*Also published in paperback by Ballantine Books.